John Cosin

Prince Bishop of Durham

Published by The Langley Press, 2020.

The author is a member of the Northumbria Area Meeting of the Religious Society of Friends (Quakers).

Pictures marked 'DCC' are printed by kind permission of Durham County Council.

to Patricia Francis

Spelling, capitalisation and some punctuation have been modernised in quotations from seventeenth-century sources.

John Cosin
Prince Bishop of Durham

Simon Webb

Also from the Langley Press

The Prince Bishops of Durham

The Dunbar Martyrs: Scottish Prisoners of War
in Durham Cathedral, 1650

The Life and Times of John Duck: Durham Celebrity

John Lilburne: Gentleman, Leveller, Quaker

In Search of the Little Count: Joseph Boruwlaski, Durham
Celebrity

Victorian Durham

The Founding of Durham

The Battle of Neville's Cross

The Lambton Worm

For free downloads and more from the Langley Press,
please visit our website at http://tinyurl.com/lpdirect

CONTENTS

Engraving of a portrait of Cosin kept at
Peterhouse College, Cambridge

Restoration

In the middle of August 1661 a bizarre ritual was re-enacted on the River Tees, probably at Neasham, a few miles to the south-east of Darlington. At the time, there were so many people and horses in the ford there that there was 'scarce any water to be seen'. The 'gentry, clergy and other people' who made up the crowd had come to see the first entry of John Cosin, the new bishop of Durham, into his diocese.

By ancient tradition, the new bishop is presented with a famous sword as he crosses the Tees either at the ford at Neasham or over the bridge at Croft-on-Tees. The sword is technically a falchion, a weapon that looks like a cross between a medieval sword and a modern machete. The sword that is handed to new bishops of Durham is the so-called Conyers falchion. It is usually presented by the lord of Sockburn, another place on the Tees, which lies a few miles to the south-east of Neasham. If the lord of Sockburn is unavailable or does not feel up to the task, his steward may present the falchion. By way of explanation, the lord or his steward should recite the following epic speech as he or she hands over the weapon:

My Lord Bishop, I here present you with the falchion wherewith the champion Conyers slew the worm, dragon, or fiery flying serpent, which destroyed man, woman, and child; in memory of which the king then reigning gave him the manor of Sockburn, to hold by this tenure, that upon the first entrance of every bishop into the country, this falchion should be presented.

When the ritual was performed for Cosin in 1661, there were 'trumpets and gunshots and acclamations'. According to a fragment of an old ballad reproduced in an 1834 book called *The Bishoprick Garland*, an earlier bishop of Durham may have been directly threatened by the Sockburn Worm:

Sockburn, - where Conyers the trusty
A huge serpent did dish up,
That had else eat the Bish-up,
But now his old falchion's grown rusty, grown rusty.

In one version of the river ritual, the incoming bishop hands the Conyers falchion back to the lord of Sockburn or his steward, while wishing the lord health and long enjoyment of his manor. At some point, however, the famous falchion came into the permanent possession of Durham Cathedral, where it is now usually to be seen among the cathedral's treasures. Although 'Conyers the trusty' is said to have killed his worm some time in the eleventh century, the falchion in the cathedral (which has certainly not 'grown rusty, grown rusty') probably dates from the thirteenth century. Its design incorporates a dragon motif, and it is possible that the 'huge serpent' story was inspired by the look of the sword itself.

The 'worm, dragon, or fiery flying serpent' 'the champion Conyers slew' was thought to have been a 'wyvern' or two-legged winged dragon. It was only one of a number of legendary beasts supposed to have terrorised the north-east of England in times past. Other creatures included the Lambton Worm, the Laidly Worm of Spindleston Heugh and Pollard's Brawn, the last a giant boar that was killed by the hero Pollard.

Cartoon knights tend to kill dragons in order to rescue damsels in distress, who might reward them by consenting to marry their rescuer. It seems that both Conyers and Pollard had less romantic rewards in mind. As we know, Conyers was granted land by 'the king then reigning': Pollard slew the giant boar so that he could

8

take its head down to Westminster to claim a similar reward from the king; but unfortunately the beast's head was stolen from him and he was forced to claim a reward from the bishop of Durham. It may be that he got more from the bishop than he would have from the monarch. From Anglo-Saxon times the bishops of Durham enjoyed a unique amount of wealth and power. They were 'prince bishops', their territory was referred to as the 'Bishopric', 'Palatinate' or 'County Palatine', and they were said to rule like petty kings between Tees and Tyne. They controlled their own law-courts, could coin their own money, raised their own armies, and sometimes even led them into battle. Many of these powers were withdrawn during the reign of Henry VIII, but in the seventeenth century the bishop of Durham was still an important landowner and a powerful figure both locally and nationally.

Of the 'gentry, clergy and other people' who were massed in such huge numbers at the ford when John Cosin arrived, some might have been there to catch their first glimpse of the new bishop. Others would have remembered him from when he was a very active local priest and canon of the cathedral earlier in the century, although they may have been intrigued to see how much he had changed in the intervening years. At sixty-six John Cosin was reportedly still tall and erect, despite years of intense study and desk-work, chronic ill-health and the very hard times he had endured in exile during the Interregnum. He had once been a strikingly good-looking man, but later portraits suggest that years of struggle had made him leaner and meaner-looking. His new bishopric was also in a bad way: as he crossed the River Tees in 1661 Cosin must have known that he had his work cut out for him.

Norwich, Cambridge and Bishop Overall

The bishop who came into possession of money, land and a great deal of power in 1661 had had a relatively humble start in life. John Cosin was born in the ancient city of Norwich on St Andrew's Day, the thirtieth of November, 1594. Norwich was then the largest city in England after London, having a population of about fifteen thousand, and John's father Giles seems to have been one of its more substantial citizens. Some sources hesitate to give Giles's profession, but in his biography of Cosin, P.H. Osmond suggests that he was a tailor, since Peter Smart, one of Cosin's Durham enemies, wrote that the future bishop 'could tell how to prick a louse in his father's shop at Norwich'. 'Prick-louse' is a derogatory nick-name for a tailor, especially popular in the north, that dates back to at least the early sixteenth century.

The surname Cosin and John's mother's maiden surname, Remington, both have quite a history in the Norwich area. A local Roger Cosyn was important enough to be involved in a legal dispute over land during the reign of Edward I (d. 1307): the same Roger Cosyn may also have been lord of the Norfolk manor of Elyngham Magna in 1314. In 1322 a John Cosyn of Norwich was granted permission by King Edward II to found a chantry in the city: this would have been a place where prayers would be offered up for the souls of the dead. As for John's mother Elizabeth, she is said to have been descended from the Remingtons of Castle Remington. St Andrew's Church, Norwich, has a monument to a Rebecca Remyngton, who died in 1604, and a communion cup donated by an Alderman Nathaniel Remyngton.

John Cosin attended the Grammar School at Norwich, near the city's cathedral. The history of this school, which still exists, can be traced back to the late eleventh century. Later alumni include Horatio Nelson and the painters Cotman and Crome. When he was only thirteen, Cosin's father died, bequeathing his eldest son several houses. John gave the rights to these to his mother, but reserved an income of twenty pounds a year from the property for himself, equivalent to around three thousand today.

The annual twenty pounds was supposed to help John through college. In 1610, at the tender age of fourteen, Cosin went to Gonville and Caius College, Cambridge. The college had important ties with Norwich, and Norfolk as a whole, and Cosin had secured one of the college's four scholarships reserved for boys from his home city.

Today such an early start at college would only be enjoyed by infant prodigies of the sort who begin coding computer software before they can even walk, but many of Cosin's contemporaries went to university when today they would not be expected to have finished school. John Overall, another future bishop who helped Cosin in his career, was only fifteen when he began to attend St John's College, Cambridge; and William Harvey, discoverer of the circulation of the blood, was the same age when he started to attend Cosin's college, Gonville and Caius. Not surprisingly, the more dedicated scholars often spent seven years at college, which must have served them as a combination of a modern upper secondary school and sixth-form centre in their early teens. His early start at Cambridge meant that John Cosin was a B.A. at eighteen.

It is to be hoped that the cash Cosin derived from his father's houses helped to spare him the privations suffered by some students at Caius in the seventeenth century. According to John Venn's history of the place, the students were rather overcrowded at times, up to four sharing one room, sometimes with their tutor making five. They were often expected to sleep on low 'truckle beds' that were stored under their tutor's bed during the day, and to study alone in cupboard-like rooms called 'studies' 'in size . . . between a sentry-box and a bathing-machine'. Poorer students might find themselves in tiny, unheated attic rooms: before bed they would 'go into the court, and walk or run up and down half an hour to get an heat in their feet'. All of them had to get up early for chapel, where the morning service commenced at the unearthly hour of five.

Although conditions might have been harsh for some, the education many received at Caius in Cosin's day was top-notch. According to Venn, who was the inventor of the Venn diagram as well as author of the college history, in the seventeenth century there were fewer 'of the sons of the great gentry and of the nobility' who, it is implied, did not really require rigorous academic training; but there were more scholarship boys who studied hard and went on to be clergymen. About seventy-five percent of Caius graduates went on to take holy orders, although the college was not particularly noted for theology. The majority stayed long enough to gain an M.A., and their number included such learned men as Cosin himself and another future bishop, Cosin's older contemporary Jeremy Taylor. The main subjects studied were rhetoric, logic and the classics.

The Master of Caius in Cosin's day was William Branthwaite, a Norfolk man like Cosin himself, who was learned enough to be one of the scholars chosen to collaborate on the translation of the Apocrypha for what became known as the King James Bible. Venn writes that 'his learning was beyond dispute, and he was known as a very able and vigilant head of the college, which flourished greatly under his rule'.

Branthwaite, who died of tuberculosis in 1619, 'left money for the foundation of additional scholarships, as also plate, and a very large and valuable collection of books'. With a true scholar's concern for the fate of his library, Branthwaite arranged for his books to be inspected once a year – something modern library staff might call an annual stock-take. When John Cosin built his own library at Durham, he provided for an elaborate annual inspection of the stock. Apparently Branthwaite's book bequest to Caius was so large that a separate catalogue had to be established for it. It included books on theology, philosophy and classical literature, sixty of them early printed books published before 1520.

Cosin's old college, which was founded in 1348, had had a purpose-built library since 1441, and a catalogue was compiled under the then master of the college, John Caius, in 1569. The first librarian was appointed in 1629. Books and libraries were to play an important part in John Cosin's career, and his love of books was one of his more likeable characteristics. It is likely that it was at Caius that the future bishop got his first taste of what a really great library could be.

Around 1616, when he was about twenty years of age, Cosin got the kind of job-offer many scholars dream of – the chance to be in charge of an extensive library; in this case the collection of a leading bishop. In Cosin's case, the remarkable thing is that two different bishops made him the same offer – Lancelot Andrewes, then bishop of Ely, and John Overall, bishop of Lichfield. After consulting with his tutor, John Browne, Cosin decided to go with Overall. He not only took charge of the bishop's library – he also acted as the man's secretary, for which position his excellent handwriting made him particularly suitable. Thanks in part to the books to which Cosin now had access, he was able to continue studying while he was in Overall's employ – the bishop advised him to study divinity.

Overall had been a professor of divinity, master of St Catherine's College, Cambridge, dean of St Paul's Cathedral and one of Queen Elizabeth I's chaplains. It seems that he was so used to lecturing in Latin that he found it 'troublesome' to preach a sermon in English. Like William Branthwaite, Overall was asked to help out with the King James Version, working under Lancelot Andrewes on the first books of the Old Testament. In 1618 Overall became bishop of Cosin's home city of Norwich, but died just over a year later.

Theologically, Overall voiced doubts about the idea of predestination, which was then associated with Calvinism and Puritanism. In 1595 the then archbishop of Canterbury, John Whitgift, had drawn up the nine so-called Lambeth Articles, designed to clarify the Church of England's position on this tricky theological issue. The Articles asserted, among other things, that everyone is predestined to either life (meaning eternal life in heaven, after the death of their earthly body) or death (meaning eternity in hell). Those predestined for life are referred to in the Articles as the elect: these lucky people have been predestined in this way for all eternity; the number of the elect has also been fixed for all eternity. Perhaps the bleakest aspect of this rather grim set of ideas, as expressed in the Lambeth Articles, is the notion that 'it is not in everyone's will and power to be saved' (Article nine): in other words, when you're damned you're damned, and there's nothing you can do about it. By the same token, it is also impossible make a u-turn on your predestined route to heaven, if you happen to be heading that way, since 'the true faith of the elect never fails finally nor totally' (Article five).

Thinkers like John Overall found the idea of predestination as set out in statements like the Lambeth Articles rather hard to digest: he argued, for instance, that someone whom the church and his own conscience had convinced was one of the elect could surely lose that status by, for instance, committing adultery. And couldn't someone who was considered to be predestined to hell save himself from the fire by a reformed life and sincere repentance?

In later years, predestination and related issues would become a serious bone of contention between churchmen like Overall and Cosin and their opponents on the Puritan, Calvinist wing of the Church of England.

London, Durham and the *Private Devotions*

John Cosin always referred to his old patron Bishop Overall with the greatest respect. Unfortunately this gifted prelate died in 1619, but his protégé soon found himself working for another bishop, Richard Neile of Durham. By this time, Cosin must have taken holy orders, as he became a private chaplain to the bishop.

Neile was a very different animal from Overall. He had no great pretensions to learning himself, admitting that he had been 'counted an heavy-headed lubber' at school, though he was able to recognise and appreciate learning in others. Despite his intellectual deficiencies, which meant that he had frequently been flogged as a schoolboy at Westminster, as a clergyman Neile managed to assemble a great many lucrative livings. In keeping with the typical practice of the time in the Church of England, Neile was able to benefit from the incomes to be derived from these livings and other appointments without doing much if any of the work associated with them. Like many English clergymen, well into the nineteenth century, including John Cosin himself, Neile employed curates and other deputies to 'cover' for him while he enriched himself financially. It was also completely normal at this time for clergymen and other officials to succeed to livings and other preferments via the influence of their friends and relatives.

Neile also became a royal chaplain and friend of King James I, and went on to be the first married dean of Westminster. From 1608 Cosin's new master held a record six different sees as bishop or archbishop: Rochester, Lichfield and Coventry, Lincoln, Durham (1617-28) and Winchester. In 1632, Neile became archbishop of York, one of the two Church of England archbishops (the other is of course the archbishop of Canterbury).

As bishop of Durham, Neile was able to take possession of Durham House, the bishop's palace on the Strand in London. Built by Bishop Hatfield in the fourteenth century, this was evidently a large place, with windows overlooking the Thames. Neile and his wife Dorothy turned it into a comfortable but stimulating home-from-home in the English capital for his friends and followers, including Cosin, and the future archbishop of Canterbury William Laud. Another associate of both Neile and Cosin was Richard Mountague, a controversial opponent of the Puritanism that was then becoming more and more important in English Christianity. Cosin said that Mountague's writings stood 'in the gap against Puritanism and popery, the Scylla and Charybdis of ancient piety'. Mountague's 1625 book *Appello Caesarem* proved extremely controversial, and attracted the attention of Parliament. Neile and Cosin were among those who defended its author, who later became bishop of Chichester, and then of Cosin's home city, Norwich.

Mountague had deliberately embroiled himself in the paper- or pamphlet-wars that were such a feature of the seventeenth century in England. These saw authors attacking each other, often on religious grounds, sometimes in badly-printed pamphlets or short books, many of which had ridiculously long titles. Some of these publications were widely read and discussed: what today seem like disputes over obscure theological matters were more important to readers then, partly because religion and politics were so tightly bound together. Sometimes it was impossible to understand a tract of the time without having read the earlier tract that it was designed to answer: in answer to a tract called *A Gag for the New Gospel*, Mountague wrote another called *A Gag for the New Gospel? No: a New Gag for an Old Goose* (1624).

Neile, Cosin, Laud and others formed the Durham House group, an influential clique that opposed aspects of Puritanism and Calvinism, looked back with respect at the ideas of men like John Overall, and became associated with Arminianism, inspired by the Dutch Theologian Jacobus Arminius (1560-1609).

Arminius had been particularly opposed to the Calvinist idea of predestination, but members of the Durham House group were also keen on elaborate church ritual, with fine church music and attention to visual aspects such as church architecture and decorations, and the vestments worn by priests. Cosin's Durham House associates therefore opposed the plainness of the Puritan way of doing things, and emphasised ritual over preaching, sermons and lectures: they believed in 'the beauty of holiness'.

Such views naturally exposed the Durham House divines to the accusation that they were aping the ways of the Roman Catholics, or were even Roman Catholics in disguise. Such accusations had been hurled at various men associated with Gonville and Caius, Cosin's old college, long before John ever set foot in the place. On one occasion, the rooms occupied by John Caius, re-founder and master of the college, had been ransacked by intruders looking for evidence of his supposed Roman Catholicism. In those days, Roman Catholics were regarded with a great deal of hostile suspicion, and were cruelly persecuted in England. In 1594, the year of John Cosin's birth, the Roman Catholic martyr John Boste was publicly butchered outside the city of Durham, simply because he was an English Roman Catholic priest who had dared to return to his home country.

Neither Bishop Neile nor his chaplain John Cosin could spend all of their time in London. Neile turned out to be a very active bishop of Durham, though many resented his presence and his actions. Around the time he was confirmed as bishop, there happened to be an unusual number of deaths among the canons of Durham, which meant that Neile could put many of his protégés into lucrative and influential positions. Cosin became one of Neile's new canons, and was also given the mastership of Greatham Hospital. This was not a hospital in the modern sense, but rather an almshouse, or what we might now call 'sheltered accommodation'; in this case for elderly and infirm people. Greatham had been founded in 1273 by Robert de Sitchell, another of the powerful prince-bishops of Durham; but for some reason Cosin quickly swapped his mastership for the rectorship of Elwick. Other preferments enjoyed by Cosin included the position of archdeacon of the East Riding of Yorkshire, and the rectorship of

Brancepeth. In typical seventeenth century style, Cosin probably gained this additional rectory because of his friendship with the aforementioned William Laud, and Laud's friend George Villiers, first duke of Buckingham, who was in turn a great favourite of King Charles I.

Although Cosin called it 'a remote and quiet place', Brancepeth is only a few miles to the south-west of Durham City, and is well worth a visit. The village boasts a castle that would be an excellent choice of location for any film or TV drama set in the Arthurian universe; and also St Brandon's church, in which Cosin installed what Osmond calls 'an abundance of woodwork which can hardly be exceeded in richness in any village church in England'. Unfortunately Cosin's beautiful, elaborate woodwork was destroyed in a fire in 1998, along with the church's roof. Luckily Cosin's stone porch, which Osmond finds 'somewhat incongruous', can still be seen. Cosin was often to be found at Brancepeth when he was not required in London or Durham, or at the bishop of Durham's palace, Auckland Castle at Bishop Auckland.

John Cosin now considered himself to be sufficiently well-established in his career to marry. It is tempting to characterise his August 1626 marriage to Frances Blakiston as yet another career- and status-enhancing move, however. Frances was a daughter of the influential Blakiston family of Newton Hall near Durham, of whom Surtees, the celebrated historian of Durham, says 'few families of private gentry have spread more widely, or flourished fairer, than Blakiston'.

Marmaduke Blakiston, Cosin's new father-in-law, was another of those seventeenth-century clergyman who were called 'pluralists' because they benefited from the incomes of many positions that he held 'in plurality'; in his case more positions than he could possibly have held if he had ever attempted to do all of the work they entailed. It was Marmaduke who had passed the job of archdeacon of the East Riding to Cosin. He also managed to pass his positions as a canon of Durham Cathedral and rector of Sedgefield to his own son Robert.

Although the eminent position he had climbed to by his early thirties would be untenable by modern standards, John Cosin was by no means an idle fat-cat. There was much for him to do, especially in his role as archdeacon of the East Riding. Churches and other buildings had been allowed to fall into disrepair, many priests were negligent in their duties, and some had not even been ordained by a bishop; or had come into their positions by corrupt means. In response to these challenges, Cosin seems to have been very conscientious and assiduous, while at the same time indulging his bookish and antiquarian tendencies in a useful way. He took on the task of hunting through the masses of property deeds kept in carefully labelled boxes in the Durham Cathedral treasury, and comparing them to the *Repertorium Magnum*, a fifteenth-century Latin catalogue that is still extant.

While he was rooting around in the cathedral treasury, Cosin did not neglect the library. In 1628 he drew up an Act of Chapter providing 'for the replenishing and maintaining' of the library, which still exists, in the cause of 'the advancement of religion and learning'.

Cosin's bookishness was also a factor in his completion of what some regard as one of his greatest achievements, which others, however, saw as a serious mistake and even an offence. The story is told by the famous diarist John Evelyn (1620-1706) and has to do with the fact that King Charles I had married Princess Henrietta Maria, a French Roman Catholic:

The Queen coming over into England, with a great train of French ladies, they were often upbraiding our English ladies of the court, that, having so much leisure, trifled away their time in the antechambers among the young gallants, without having something to divert themselves of more devotion; whereas the Roman Catholic ladies had their hours and breviaries, which entertained them in religious exercise. Our Protestant ladies, scandalized at this reproach, it was complained of to the king. Whereupon his majesty called Bishop White to him, and asked his thoughts of it, and whether there might not be found some form of prayers amongst the ancient liturgies proper on this occasion, that so the court ladies might at least appear as devout as the new come-over French. The bishop told the king it might certainly be done, and believed it very

19

necessary: whereupon his majesty immediately commanded him to employ some person of the clergy to set upon the work, and compose an office of that nature. The bishop presently named Dr Cosin, (whom the king exceedingly approved of) to prepare, as speedily as he could, and as like to their pocket offices, as he could with regard to the ancient forms before popery.

This all happened in 1627: Evelyn's account is interesting because it shows that by this time Cosin was already 'exceedingly approved of' by the king, and that both King Charles and Bishop Francis White of Carlisle considered Cosin the right man to be asked to draw up what became Cosin's *Collection of Private Devotions*; although White was a noted author and might have been up to the task himself.

'Their hours' as referred to by Evelyn were the so-called books of hours used by Roman Catholics as aids to private prayer. Illuminated medieval examples of such books are among the most beautiful manuscript volumes ever produced in the west. The early fifteenth century French *Très Riches Heures* of the Duc de Berry is a celebrated example.

It is interesting that Charles I seemed to think that the way such a book could be produced without its appearing at all Roman Catholic, though it was supposed to be 'like to their pocket offices', would be for Cosin to search out 'the ancient forms before popery'. It is also interesting that nobody seemed to think that the Anglican Book of Common Prayer, which the English had been using for private devotion since it first appeared in the sixteenth century, was equal to the task of satisfying the queen's Protestant ladies.

The perceived need for Cosin to search out 'ancient forms' relates to an idea then current in the Church of England that the national church was not some brash new institution that had merely sprung up under Henry VIII, but was connected to an ancient form of Christianity that pre-dated the type of Roman Catholicism many English people had been taught to despise. It was important for the Church of England to make this claim of great antiquity because at that time antiquity (for instance of a family, a law or an author) was often seen as a guarantee of authenticity and value. The claim of the English Church to greater antiquity than 'popery' can easily be refuted by any Catholic, who merely has to point out that the popes are the successors of St Peter.

Though it tried to avoid seeming too Roman Catholic, especially in its later editions, Cosin's popular *Private Devotions* were quickly identified by the Puritans as further evidence that men like Cosin, King Charles, Bishop White and their associates, including Bishops Neile and Laud, were in effect Roman Catholics. Chief among the book's critics was the Puritan William Prynne (1600-1669) who made a play on Cosin's name and called the book 'Mr Cosin's cozening devotions'.

Prynne was a formidable combatant in the pamphlet-wars of the time. He was also well-educated, had had legal training and was sometimes a Member of Parliament. He was a dyed-in-the-wool Presbyterian, which meant that he opposed the very existence of bishops, though he was also an Erastian, who believed that secular rulers such as monarchs should have a lot of power over the church. Prynne lived up to the spoil-sport image of the Puritan: he got into serious trouble because his book *Histriomastix* (1632) criticised theatrical performances at a time when members of the royal family were participating in such things at court. As a punishment, Prynne had his ears cut off by the public executioner.

Peter Smart, King Charles I and Peterhouse

Shortly after Cosin's Act of Chapter calling for the replenishing of the cathedral's library was signed by the dean, Peter Smart, another of the cathedral's canons, delivered an outrageous sermon condemning, in no uncertain terms, the actions of Cosin and his associates. On the twenty-seventh of July 1628 the grey walls of Durham Cathedral resounded to Smart's voice as he railed against the new Arminian touches that had been introduced into that hallowed place since the arrival of Bishop Neile (who by this time had moved on to Winchester).

The sermon as given in the cathedral did not name Cosin, although the published version did. Here the canon's proceedings were compared to pagan rites, and the man himself was called 'our young Apollo, who repaireth the Quire and sets it out gaily with strange Babylonish ornaments'. The young god's allies among the bishops were called 'the Whore of Babylon's dastardly brood, doting upon their mother's beauty, that painted harlot of the Church of Rome', and also 'Balaams, which lay stumbling-blocks in your way, to make you fall into spiritual fornication, telling you, when you bow to the altar, you worship God, not the altar'. Smart's reference to Balaam relates to Revelation 2:14, where we are told that this Old Testament figure 'taught Balac to cast a stumblingblock before the children of Israel, to eat things sacrificed unto idols, and to commit fornication' (King James Version).

Altars and the way priests and worshippers behaved around them were a particular concern of Smart's. He had objected to the way that the communion table had been moved to the east end of the cathedral in 1617, something that struck him as too Roman Catholic. He was also displeased when the table was later replaced by an altar with black stone pillars, decorated with 'cherubim-faces, as white as snow'. He called such altars damnable idols, and the people who bowed to them 'spiritual fornicators'. He also claimed that the altar had cost three thousand pounds, though the figure was probably more like two hundred. In his inflammatory sermon, Smart described the effect he thought the new music and elaborate ceremonies were having on the minds of believers:

the sacrament itself is turned near into a theatrical stage play, that when men's minds should be occupied about heavenly meditations, of Christ's bitter death and passion, of their own sins and of faith and repentance, of the joys of heaven, and the torments of hell, their ears are possessed with pleasant tunes, and their eyes fed with pompous spectacles.

Smart advised his hearers to 'stay at home in the name of God, until such things be mended'. 'Such things' also included the use of candles and tapers. Later Cosin was accused of using no less than three hundred and forty lit candles at Candlemas, and displaying his 'hypocritical seeming holiness in upstartings, down-squattings, east-turnings, crossings and kissing altar-cloths and the elements of bread and wine, with frequent and profound duckings and prostrations before the altar'. Smart also accused Cosin of man-handling worshippers who refused to worship as he thought they should, and calling them 'pagans' and 'silly sows'.

Dean Hunt, Cosin himself, Cosin's father-in-law Marmaduke Blakiston and another canon confronted Smart in the deanery on the afternoon of the day he had delivered his sermon. Smart handed over a written copy of the sermon to be copied out, but refused to retract anything he had said in it. He was quickly deprived of the income from his position as canon, and later made unsuccessful attempts to appeal to the law and to Parliament, which only landed him in more trouble.

A second attempt to bring his case before a judge saw the judge in question, Sir Henry Yelverton, agreeing that Cosin and others might have broken the law by introducing new features into the services and decorations of Durham Cathedral. Yelverton particularly singled out the chanting of psalms as something he personally disliked; but soon the old judge relented, stopped the prosecution of the offending canons in its tracks, and tried to reconcile Smart with his colleagues.

Smart also alleged that, at a dinner at Durham in April 1628, Cosin had denied that the king was head of the church. This accusation was taken up by no less a figure than the attorney-general – a very worrying development. Cosin appealed to Laud, sending him a letter in which he explained that what he had actually said was that English monarchs were 'supreme governor both of church and state, and that by their power of supreme dominion they might command churchmen at any time to do their office, or punish them for the neglect of it', but that 'the power of spiritual jurisdiction itself was from Christ, who had given it unto his apostles, and they to their successors in ordination'.

At the dinner and in his letter to Laud, Cosin had backed up his assertion by pointing out that, though the king might indeed 'command churchmen at any time' he was not a priest, and could not, for instance, administer the sacraments, or excommunicate anyone. One reason why Cosin had made this controversial assertion was because ' the pope's flatterers' called him, the pope, the head of the church. In the end, King Charles ordered the attorney-general to drop the matter, and Peter Smart was frustrated again.

Since Smart played such an important (if very disruptive) role in John Cosin's life, it might be worthwhile to step back and take a longer view of him. He was a native of Stratford-upon-Avon in Warwickshire, where his father was vicar of William Shakespeare's home town. Like Bishop Neile, he had attended Westminster School, and he proceeded to Broadgates Hall, Oxford, and then to Christ Church, where William James, a future bishop of Durham, was master. Smart followed James to Durham when the latter became dean in 1597. He became master of Durham School, and when James became bishop of Durham in 1606 he ordained Smart, made him his chaplain and a cathedral canon, and also made him rector of Boldon. Smart also became master of St Edmund's hospital, Gateshead. Evidently, Smart thrived under Bishop James, whom he compared to Neile, calling the former 'our less ceremonious, and more preaching' bishop. In case anyone doubted his religious views, William James included a very Calvinist phrase in his will, expressing his hope 'to be received into his [meaning God's] mercy seat with the rest of his elect and chosen Israel'. Smart no doubt thought of Neile as a less preaching, and more ceremonial, bishop. In any case, Smart could not stomach the innovations Neile, Cosin and their allies introduced at Durham.

Although the power of the Puritans was becoming formidable at this time, not everybody objected to the elaborate services that had been introduced into Durham's cathedral. Three army officers who attended a service in 1634 'were wrapt with the sweet sound, and richness of a fair organ, which cost £1000, and the devout and melodious singing of the choristers'. The soldiers were also impressed with what they saw in the vestry: 'divers fair copes of several rich works, of crimson satin, embroidered with embossed work of silver, beset all over with cherubims . . .' In other words, the officers enjoyed all the things that sent Peter Smart into a towering rage. The lieutenant who was one of the 'dusty, travelling soldiers' recorded his impressions in a manuscript, which found its way into what was then the British Museum Library, and was published in 1904.

If Smart's attacks on Cosin and his associates were a low point of John's time as a canon at Durham, the visit of King Charles I to the city in June 1633 was surely a high point. On this occasion, the king was attended by his archbishop of Canterbury, William Laud, and Cosin was put in charge of the ceremonies surrounding Charles's reception in the cathedral, and the services he attended there.

The king was on his way to Scotland to be crowned king of that country; something which was long overdue. On the afternoon of June the first he entered the cathedral via the north door, under a silken canopy held up by eight canons in surplices. He was led to a chair near the font, and listened to a welcoming address from the dean. His majesty then attended a short service in the quire, and visited the tombs of St Cuthbert and the Venerable Bede. Charles was also presented with a gorgeous cope, which he handed over to Laud. The cost to the Bishop of Durham of entertaining the king was fifteen hundred pounds a day.

Two days later, the cathedral chapter received a letter from the king in which, writing from his position as head of the state church, his majesty ordered the removal of some houses that had been allowed to spring up just to the north of the cathedral 'which we cannot but think most unfitting for that place and altogether unseeming the magnificence of so godly a fabric'. In his 1973 history of the cathedral, C.J. Stranks suggested that some of these buildings probably served as homes for men paid to sing in the choir, and that one of them may have been an old office that had been turned into a song-school. In any case, the buildings King Charles mentioned were demolished later in 1633.

Charles ordered that some seats in the quire, which were being used by the mayor of Durham and certain local 'women of quality' should also be removed. It is likely that Cosin and Laud had persuaded the king to compose his letter.

1633, the year King Charles I visited Durham, was one of the years of that unhappy monarch's so-called 'personal rule'. From 1629 to 1640 Charles attempted to run England without calling any parliament. Since parliaments were a major source of income for English monarchs, Charles had to resort to unpopular measures, such as reviving crusty old forgotten taxes and fines, to raise money. This, as well as his fondness for the kind of elaborate church liturgy that John Cosin favoured, made the king very unpopular among many of his subjects.

We already know that Charles 'exceedingly approved of' John Cosin even before his distinguished visit to Durham in 1633. It seems that John's approval rating with the king went up even further after the visit: in February 1635, Cosin became master of Peterhouse, which claims to be the oldest college belonging to Cambridge University. The job had become vacant because the previous master, Matthew Wren (an uncle of Christopher Wren the architect) had been elected bishop of Hereford. Wren was, like Cosin and his associates, an opponent of Puritanism and Calvinism, and a man favoured by Charles I: indeed Wren had accompanied the king on his 1633 trip to Scotland via Durham. At Peterhouse, Wren had built a new college chapel, which was consecrated by our friend Bishop White in March 1632. The chapel was certainly not Puritan in style: Wren installed an altar at the east end, which was railed in – something the Puritans disliked. There were also altar-cloths of sumptuous materials, with sacred monograms embroidered on them in silver and gold thread.

John Cosin, the new master of Peterhouse, continued Wren's work in the chapel in much the same vein. In his 1646 book *Canterbury's Doom*, the aforementioned Puritan author William Prynne complained that 'a glorious new altar' had been set up in the Peterhouse chapel, 'to which the master, fellows, and scholars bowed and were enjoined to bow by Dr Cosin the master'. The altar was adorned with 'basins, candlesticks, tapers standing on it, and a great crucifix hanging over it'. There were also 'pictures of the Holy Ghost in form of a dove', and 'there was likewise a carved cross at the end of every seat'. Everybody had to make 'a low obeisance to the altar, being enjoined by Dr Cosin under a penalty (as they reported) to do it'. According to Prynne, many scholars attended the services, some of them from other colleges, 'some out of curiosity only to behold, others to learn and practise the popish ceremonies and orders used in that chapel'.

As well as imposing a penalty on people who did not bow to the altar, Cosin made sure that students over eighteen who missed prayers without good reason were fined, and that offenders under eighteen were deprived of dinner or supper. The owner of any dog that strayed into the chapel was also to be fined five shillings.

Cosin also reported back to the archbishop of Canterbury, William Laud, on any objectionable goings-on in other college chapels and churches, including the use of 'profane and scurrilous jests', and the misuse of such spaces for storage of, for instance, scaffolding, cupboards and book binders' equipment. Cosin also reported on sloppy, haphazard services and the use of extempore prayers: he was assisted in the compilation of these reports by

Richard Sterne, then master of Jesus College, and great-grandfather of Laurence Sterne, author of *Tristram Shandy*. As vice-chancellor of the university Cosin also beautified the university church of Great St Mary, and, according to William Prynne, introduced 'altars, crucifixes, candlesticks, tapers, and bowing to altars'.

Given his marked interest in books, the new master was bound to turn his attention to the Peterhouse college library, which by his time was already housed in a purpose-built structure, and had over five hundred medieval manuscripts among its treasures. Cosin contributed around eight hundred more books, including some important volumes of church music. He also installed some new book-cases, and provided for the income of a librarian. As vice-chancellor, Cosin also tried to have a university library built, but, like much else, this project was frustrated by the alarming political developments of the 1640s.

A Hostile Environment

Peter Smart's attempt to bring down Cosin and his allies had left him in prison and out of pocket. Smart was not, however, the kind of man to stay beaten, and in November 1640 he again presented a petition to Parliament, complaining of Cosin's 'popish' innovations and his own ill-treatment at the hands of the law. Luckily for Cosin, this parliament was the aptly-named Short Parliament, which only sat for three weeks in 1640. King Charles had called the parliament hoping that it might help him raise money for his wars against the Scots.

These were the Bishops' Wars of 1639 and 1640, which had been provoked by Charles's insistence that the Scots should accept bishops and abandon Presbyterianism, a form of church government that is quite innocent of bishops. Unfortunately for Charles, the members of the Short Parliament were more interested in criticising their king than voting him money, so his majesty dissolved the parliament on the fifth of May 1640. This only provided a temporary respite for Cosin, however.

One consequence of the Bishops' Wars was that under the terms of the Treaty of Ripon (signed in October 1640) Scottish troops were permitted to occupy Northumberland and County Durham. The English even agreed to pay the Scots eight hundred and fifty pounds a day for the privilege of having parts of their country occupied. This amount would be worth over a hundred thousand pounds today, and the extra expenditure was one reason why Charles had to recall Parliament again, in November 1640.

Thus began the Long Parliament, which continued for twenty years.

The then bishop of Durham, Thomas Morton, as well as the dean and others, fled before the Scots, and certain indispensable records and portable treasures were moved south to Hull. Some of the revenues of the cathedral were used to contribute to the invaders' daily eight hundred and fifty pounds. It now became difficult for people like John Cosin to gain access to the revenues they were used to getting from various sources in Durham and elsewhere in the north of England. As a result, Cosin had to live on the forty pounds a year he earned as master of Peterhouse. To plug the gap in his finances, in November 1640 Cosin was made dean of Peterborough, thanks to Archbishop Laud's influence with the king. This shows how the system was working in Cosin's favour, but this state of affairs, the new dean of Peterborough's career, and the system itself, were all teetering on the edge of one of history's precipices at this time.

Just seven days after the Long Parliament began to meet in November 1640, Peter Smart presented his grievances to the House. Given the Puritan sympathies of many of the members, Smart was almost guaranteed a sympathetic hearing. He alleged that Cosin stood to the east of the table when celebrating holy communion, that he covered cushions and benches with crosses, that he had criticised some of the instigators of the Protestant Reformation, and that he denied the royal supremacy over the church. The last was of course an old charge (based on reports of that fateful 1628 dinner in Durham) of which Cosin had been cleared years before.

Although Cosin attempted to deny all of Smart's charges, he soon found himself in the custody of Parliament's sergeant-at-arms. A committee was appointed to look into the charges against him: meanwhile he was released on bail. When he was called to appear before a committee, Cosin bowed to them. 'Here is no altar, Dr Cosin,' commented some waggish member of the committee, referring to Cosin's controversial practice of bowing to the altar. 'Why then,' Cosin replied, 'I hope there shall be no sacrifice'.

Three days later the committee reported that Smart's allegations were founded on truth, and that Cosin himself was 'unfit and unworthy to be a governor in either of the universities, or to continue any longer head or governor of any college, or to hold or enjoy any ecclesiastical promotions'. The committee's findings were sent up to the House of Lords, and plans were laid to impeach Cosin. In March 1641 Francis Rous, the Puritan head of the committee that had looked into Smart's allegations, addressed the House of Lords. In his speech, Rous called Peter Smart 'a protomartyr or first confessor of note in the late days of persecution', putting him on a par with St Alban, the protomartyr or first martyred saint of the British, who was executed in the city that now bears his name, in Roman times.

Rous went on to paint a lurid picture of 'an army of priests with a great design of bringing popery', in which Cosin was supposed to be a foot-soldier. This reminds one of deluded modern conspiracy theories, which insist, for instance, that the Jews are bent on world domination, that there is a shadowy 'deep state' in America that works to frustrate the efforts of the U.S. president, or that many of the most powerful people on the planet are not originally from planet Earth at all. Such wild notions often gain currency among people who find that they fit neatly into their own world view, and if Cosin and his cronies really had been secret Roman Catholics it would certainly have been convenient for Puritans like Rous and Smart.

'This army of priests,' Rous told the Lords, 'doth many ways advance the design and plots of popery,' and he went on to describe how he imagined Cosin and his ilk were undermining the government and the Protestant religion by subverting the law, bringing in 'the pope's furniture, altars and copes, pictures and images' and punishing their enemies with 'suspension, sequestration, excommunication, degradation, and deprivation', as they were supposed to have done in Smart's case.

The judgement of the Lords had to be delayed because the Durham Cathedral records that they needed to consult had either been destroyed by the Scots, or lost on the way to Hull. When Cosin was finally allowed to speak in his own defence, he claimed that the sumptuous altar Smart objected to had been introduced before he, John Cosin, 'ever saw the country' of Durham, and that in any case the altar had not cost 'the tenth part of what is pretended, appurtenances and all'. The gorgeous copes Smart criticised likewise pre-dated Cosin, were not as expensive as Smart claimed, and, the accounts revealed, had been paid for in part by Smart himself. Cosin also implied that embroidered copes that included 'the picture of the trinity, or the image of God the father in the figure of an old man, or otherwise' were mere figments of Smart's imagination, and that he, Cosin, only ever wore a cope 'of plain white satin only, without any embroidery upon it at all' when he celebrated communion.

According to Cosin, 'the image of Christ with a blue cap and a golden beard' that Smart objected to 'was nothing else but the top of Bishop Hatfield's tomb'; and he also insisted that Smart had greatly exaggerated the number of candles used in the cathedral 'upon candlemas night or any other'. Before the Lords, Cosin went on to clear up certain other matters, at least to his own satisfaction, and identified Smart's original sermon preached against him as 'scandalous and seditious'.

In the face of Cosin's oratory, Smart's case collapsed, and, as Cosin himself recorded, his enemy's own lawyer, a Mr Glover, 'openly at the bar of that honourable House forsook him, and told him plainly that he was ashamed of his complaint and could not in conscience plead for him any longer'. The outcome was not, however, entirely disastrous for Peter Smart. He was restored to his vicarage at Aycliffe, and became once again a canon of Durham Cathedral. A charge brought against Cosin in the House of Commons, that he had converted a Mr Nicholas, fellow of Peterhouse, to Roman Catholicism, was thrown out in a similar fashion when Cosin showed that he had made Nicholas read out a recantation, and had then had him expelled from the university.

As well as Peter Smart, John Cosin's critics at this time included the authors of satirical pamphlets, including *Lambeth Fair*, a 1641 satire in doggerel verse where Cosin may be meant by a 'grave doctor' who has lost his nerve and wants to sell his slippers:

It now beginning to grow towards night,
Comes a grave Doctor running in with might;
His courage stout was somewhat now abated,
He brings his golden slippers consecrated,
And cries, 'Come buy these slippers here of mine,
They are emboss'd with holiness divine.'

In another satire called *The Doctor's Last Will and Testament* Cosin is represented as bequeathing 'my mass, popish, and Romish books, of which I have many volumes, partly to the poor that they may warm their fingers this following winter by them on the market-hill and partly to tobacconists and grocers' and 'my pictures and images partly to the apple-mongers, and partly to husbandmen, that they may be hanged up to scare crows'.

While Cosin was battling to save his career, his reputation and his way of life, his wife lost a battle of her own. She died, shortly after having given birth to a daughter, in March 1642. Meanwhile throughout the country people were preparing for another kind of battle. In August, King Charles I declared war on the parliamentarians, and Britain's seventeenth-century civil wars began in earnest.

Having avoided punishment following the accusations made against himself and his associates by Peter Smart, Cosin put himself firmly in the wrong, at least from the Roundhead point of view, by attempting to send money and college plate from Cambridge to the embattled king's royal mint, also in August 1642. The money included a hundred pounds from Cosin himself and another hundred from the fellows of Peterhouse.

Unfortunately for the king, this gift or loan was intercepted by a troop of volunteers commanded by one Oliver Cromwell, who was then member of parliament for Cambridge. In March 1644 Cosin was ejected from his mastership of Peterhouse. At this time, so many heads of colleges were being replaced that William Sancroft, a future archbishop of Canterbury, complained that whole colleges were being 'beheaded' at a blow.

By the time Cosin was ejected from Peterhouse, it is likely that he had already fled abroad, perhaps disguised as a miller. Meanwhile, officially-sanctioned vandals made sure that Peterborough Cathedral and the chapel at Peterhouse were stripped of the features that had been so objectionable to the Puritans. At Peterborough a group commanded by Oliver Cromwell's own son spent a fortnight destroying stained glass, choir-stalls, organs and the altar-screen, riddling a painting of Jesus with shot. They also tore up prayer-books and a bible. William Dowsing, one of the Peterhouse vandals, recorded that they 'pulled down two mighty great angels with wings, and divers other angels, and the four evangelists, and Peter with the keys over the chapel door, and about a hundred cherubims and angels, and divers superstitious letters in gold'.

Exile

It is not clear exactly when John Cosin went into exile, but it is known that he spent seventeen years abroad, mostly in Paris. That was where King Charles I's French Roman Catholic queen Henrietta Maria had already begun her own long exile. The French royal family had given her quarters in the Louvre (where she had been born in 1609) and a daily allowance of cash. Cosin was appointed by her husband Charles I as chaplain to her Protestant servants, who then greatly outnumbered her Catholic followers. It was of course the Protestant ladies of the queen's court for whom Cosin had written his *Collection of Private Devotions* in 1627. He was paid a small income and housed in the Louvre himself. A room was provided there for services, and on Sundays Cosin officiated at the chapel of the English ambassador, Sir Richard Browne. This chapel in the Faubourg St Germain became, in effect, the headquarters of the kind of English Christianity Cosin stood for. It was also in this chapel that the celebrated diarist John Evelyn was married, in 1647, to Browne's daughter Mary.

Today the Louvre is one of the great museums of the world, but in Cosin's time it was a royal palace, and less than half the size it is today. The bulk of it comprised a long range of buildings running parallel to the Seine, which had been greatly extended by Henrietta Maria's father, the French King Henri IV. The sixteenth-century Tuileries Palace, which was demolished in the nineteenth century, was another long, thin building, that stuck out at a right-angle from the Seine. It would have been obvious to Cosin that ideally, these buildings would have formed two sides of a courtyard, but the courtyard was never fully enclosed until late in the nineteenth century. The loss of the Tuileries Palace meant that the courtyard was opened out again on its west side, so that today two long wings of the Louvre seem to embrace the eastern end of the Tuileries gardens.

Although her royal father greatly extended the Louvre, so that it connected with the Tuileries Palace, and although Henrietta Maria herself was born there, Henri IV seems not to have made much use of the place as a residence. The Louvre and the Tuileries Palace in particular would have had some bad associations for him, and, later, for the Protestant members of the English court in exile. The palace had been the home of Catherine de' Medici (1519-1589), an Italian-born queen of France, who was thought by many to have had a leading role in planning the St Bartholomew's day massacres of 1572. These began in Paris just after Henrietta Maria's father, then King Henri III of Navarre and a Protestant, married his first wife, Catherine's daughter Margaret (Henrietta Maria was his child by his second wife, *Marie* de' Medici).

When the violence spread beyond the French capital, as many as thirty thousand French Protestants may have been slaughtered. According to an account published in English in 1844, 'the streets [of Paris] were covered with dead bodies, the river was tinged with blood, the doors and entrances into the king's palace were smeared with it'. In the cool of the evening, Catherine de' Medici stepped out with her royal son and the ladies of the court to view the corpses. If nothing else, the massacres gave European Protestants a historic atrocity that they could continue to use as propaganda against Roman Catholics for centuries.

In some of his sermons preached at Paris, Cosin criticised Roman Catholicism, and in others he cast shade on the types of Protestantism with which he disagreed. He was very concerned that, in the overwhelmingly Catholic atmosphere of Paris, some of the English exiles might be tempted to convert. Cosin himself wrote that he 'found many of the Roman profession (both priests and others) very busy and industrious in persuading them of our religion that attended at the English court to turn papists'.

One of these 'busy and industrious' people was Father Robinson, prior of the English Benedictine monks in France, who had made some headway in converting an English lady. The unknown lady summoned Cosin to the court, where he was asked to debate with Father Robinson on the subject of the validity of Church of England ordinations: in other words, Cosin had to maintain the position that Church of England priests were valid, genuine priests, although the Catholics of the time found it hard to accept this. The lady promised that if Cosin was beaten in the debate, she would go over to the Catholic side.

The dean was understandably reluctant to participate in this high-stakes game, because he considered the lady's promise 'too rashly and inconsiderately made, for the weight of this cause ought not to depend upon me or any other particular man'. But he consented at last, 'to preserve that person in our own communion', and debated with Robinson in front of witnesses for three or four hours. Cosin claimed to have won the debate: the opinion and the later actions of the unknown lady who provoked it are not known. In a similar debate, Cosin was matched with a 'very weary' priest who called in a couple of extra scholars to help out. Cosin claimed victory in this engagement as well, his triumph being based in part on the classic assertion that many key Catholic ideas were innovations, and that the Church of England was returning to a more ancient form of Christianity.

In another debate, Cosin and another Church of England divine disputed with a friar in the presence of a cousin of John Evelyn who had gone over to Rome. This debate happened in the house of the English ambassador, although Cosin had wanted it to take place at the Louvre, where Evelyn says the dean 'had a competent library upon occasion'. The venue had to be changed, however, for fear of offending the queen, whose chapel was nearby.

Cosin not only argued against Catholicism in sermons and public debates, but in his writings at this time, and he claimed, in 1648, that after four years not one member of the English court had become a Catholic, 'unless it were a poor footman (whom they trapped with a female French bait too)'.

Among the English who were sharing exile with Cosin and the queen at this time was the philosopher Thomas Hobbes (1588-1679). The author of *Leviathan* was appointed to teach mathematics to the future King Charles II, who arrived in Paris in 1646. Hobbes was thought of by some as a religious sceptic and an enemy to conventional morality, but it 1647 the thinker was gravely ill and forced to keep to his bed for six months. Cosin visited him as part of his priestly duty to visit the sick, and Hobbes did not reject his attentions: quite the opposite. In the Latin autobiography he sent to his friend the biographer John Aubrey, Hobbes, writing about himself in the third person, sought to disprove the charge of atheism that had been directed against him by referring to 'his confession to Dr John Cosin, at [Paris] on his (as he thought) death-bed, [when he] declared that he liked the religion of the Church of England best of all other' (trans. William Duggan, 2014).

The impact of the news of King Charles I's execution on the royalist exiles in January 1649 can only be imagined. One effect on the widowed queen, Henrietta Maria, was that she was now free of her husband's influence, and could pursue her own Roman Catholic agenda. When her son the future King James II arrived in February 1649, she set about trying to convert him, but for the moment he remained loyal to the Church of England. Soon the use of the room in the Louvre that had been set aside for Church of England services was withdrawn, though the services were allowed to continue in a private house. According to Osmond, the Catholic clergy of France attempted to raise a pension for Henrietta Maria, in response to her promise to 'gradually rid her court of all 'heretics''. Certainly the queen dismissed some of her ladies in waiting because they would not convert.

Henrietta Maria also sought to undermine Cosin by depriving him of his income. Sir Edward Nicholas, secretary of state to both Charlses, wrote that 'they' were attempting to starve out 'their parson', in the hope that 'the congregation will dissolve quietly'. Cosin himself complained that his poverty, which sometimes saw him living on sixpence a day, had made him 'as lean as Lent', though he did receive gifts of money from, among others, the aforementioned John Evelyn. Later, back in England in 1663, Evelyn complained to his diary that although he had 'assisted' Cosin in his exile, the bishop of Durham 'little remembered' this 'in his greatness'. Osmond suggests that Cosin's coldness towards

Evelyn may have been rooted in the bishop's memory of a serious attempt made by Evelyn, when they were both in France, to take advantage of the dean's poverty to buy his library from him at a knock-down price, although much of the library in question would still have been in Cambridge at the time.

Despite the poverty of his exile, it seems that John Cosin was still able to collect books. Many of these found their way into the library Cosin founded, which still stands on Palace Green in Durham. The library includes five hundred and eighty-five volumes in French, many of them so rare that even the French national library does not have copies. Richard Gameson's 2007 book *Treasures of Durham University Library* spotlights a printed book in French of which no other copy is known to exist anywhere. This comprises a poem published in 1649, the year of King Charles I's execution, by a lady called Isabeau Bernard de Lagnes, on the subject of Charles's 'mort ignominieuse'. The book is dedicated to Queen Henrietta Maria, and it is likely that the copy was given to Cosin, perhaps by the queen herself.

John Ward, who, as Peter Smart's father had been, was vicar of Stratford-upon-Avon, wrote that when Dr Cosin was in France 'divers gentlemen that travelled thitherto used to come to see him and drop some pence into his hand'. From 1654 onwards Cosin's daughter Mary, who had stayed in England, also worked hard to try to extract income due to the family from Peterhouse, Brancepeth and elsewhere. Ward revealed, however, that 'when [Cosin] was so low he was often tempted to turn papist, with large promises that if he would do so, he and his children would be provided for, and they should never trouble him more'.

Although Cosin and, for a while, the future King James II held out, Cosin's son John succumbed and was received into the Catholic communion. Here again John Evelyn enters Cosin's story. The diarist recorded that in December 1651 the younger John Cosin, who had been 'debauched by the priests, wrote a letter to me to mediate for him with his father'. According to Evelyn, the young man had fallen into the hands of the Jesuits because his father had sent him to a Jesuit college to learn Latin grammar. Both Osmond and Ornsby find this unlikely, given the evidence that

John attended the cathedral school at Peterborough (George Ornsby edited two volumes of texts relating to Cosin in the 1860s, and wrote useful biographical introductions). In any case, according to Evelyn, John junior's letter contained 'a great deal of stuff dictated by the Jesuits to justify his conversion (as they called it)'. Evelyn wrote a reply to it, a copy of which he caused to be 'purposely dropped in the queen's bed-chamber'. Cosin later wrote to Evelyn, thanking him for the letter he had written in reply to his son, a copy of which the dean showed to King Charles II. Cosin wanted to publish Evelyn's letter, but Charles warned that this might offend the queen. The dean did manage to reclaim his son for the Church of England, but this proved temporary: he converted to Catholicism again shortly after the Restoration.

While the queen was exerting influence on the Roman Catholic side, the exiled Charles II was planning to recover his kingdom with the help of the Scots. Since the Presbyterians had the upper hand north of the border, Charles felt obliged to swear to the Covenant and throw in his lot with them. This led to rumours that the young king might put a stop to the more traditional Church of England services Cosin was keen to perpetuate, and also to use of the Book of Common Prayer. Something like this – or even more extreme – might actually have happened if the Scots had had it all their own way at a conference at Breda in the Netherlands in March 1650.

In return for their help recovering his kingdom, the Scottish delegates demanded that the exiled king not only swear to the Covenant, thus committing himself to support Presbyterianism, but also to establish Presbyterianism as the dominant form of worship in England and Ireland. He was also to forbid any other form of worship in his own household: this would have meant that the queen mother would have had to abandon her Roman Catholicism, or detach herself from the English royal court altogether. If Cosin had not embraced Presbyterianism at this time, he would also have been cast out into the wilderness. Luckily for Cosin and other adherents to the Arminian and pro-bishop side of the Church of England, Charles managed to win the Scots' cooperation without actually making England and Ireland Presbyterian countries.

Although many English royalists continued to dislike Presbyterianism, and were horrified that Charles had sworn to the Scottish Covenant, in France Cosin himself established cordial relations with the Huguenots, French Protestants who had also abandoned the idea of bishops. Despite the Huguenots' lack of bishops, Cosin and others were happy to participate in services at their church at Charenton, and Huguenots were welcome at English services in Paris. Deceased members of Cosin's flock were buried in the Huguenots' cemetery at Charenton, which was fortunate because otherwise, as Cosin wrote in a letter, 'we should be forced to bury our dead in a ditch'. Cosin even baptised a number of Huguenot children, and officiated at the marriages of Huguenot couples. Some Frenchmen were even ordained as deacons or priests by exiled English bishops.

Jean Durel, a native of the Channel island of Jersey, was presented by Cosin for ordination in Sir Richard Browne's chapel in Paris. Durel later translated the 1662 edition of the Book of Common Prayer, which Cosin had helped to prepare, into French for the benefit of French-speaking Channel islanders. Jean also became a canon of Durham Cathedral when Cosin was bishop there, and, as we shall see, had a hand in preparing a Latin version of the 1662 Book of Common Prayer.

John Cosin's work to keep his own vision of the Church of England alive in exile must have involved frequent references to the then current Book of Common Prayer, the use of which was officially banned in England itself at this time. The Anglicans in exile had to rely on treasured old copies of the Prayer Book. Mary, the lady John Evelyn had married in Sir Richard Browne's chapel, had to make do with a miniature 1637 version of the book. Her father, Sir Richard Browne himself, owned an Elizabethan edition, published in 1559, which he had had re-bound in Paris.

As well as making friends with the French Protestants, Cosin enjoyed what must have been some absorbing conversations with a man he called 'the venerable prelate Cyril, archbishop of Trapezond' (now Trabzon in Turkey). Cyril visited Cosin at the Louvre and at the Palais Royal, and their discussions confirmed Cosin in his opinion that the Church of England had returned to a more ancient and venerable form of Christianity than that followed by the Roman Catholics, who had introduced 'many novelties' that the Greek Orthodox churches had never been able to accept. This particular archbishop of Trapezond or Trebizon later travelled to Rome and became a Roman Catholic himself. Years later, when Cosin was bishop of Durham, he was charitable enough to pay the living expenses of a Greek Orthodox priest who was too poor, old or infirm to make the journey from England back to his own country.

Cosin's contacts with the Huguenots and an Orthodox archbishop seem to have been genuine ecumenical efforts: such work still continues today in the Church of England, which is in dialogue with various churches large and small all over the world, and enjoys membership of ecumenical groups such as the World Council of Churches and the Global Christian Forum. In 2014 Anglican dialogue with the Oriental Orthodox churches resulted in a joint statement on Christology: the question of exactly who or what Jesus was or is.

Woodwork in Brancepeth Church before the fire

Cosin's porch at Brancepeth

I hate them that hould of superstitious vanities but thy law dee I loue Psal:31:6.7

Ætatis suæ 73 A 1641

The liuely portrature of the Reuerend Peter Smart M: of Artes
minister of Gods word at Bouden Prebend of Durham, & one of his
ma:tie High Comissioners in the prouince of Yorke, who for prea:
ching against Popery A:no 1628 lost aboue 300li: popan:u, and
was imprisoned in ye K:s bench aboue a 11 yeares by the High Comison

Peter preach donne vaine rites with flagrant harte
Thy Guerdon shall be greate, though heare thou Smart
Georg: Abbot: archepisco: Cant composuit

Cosin's enemy, Peter Smart

Richard Baxter (National Library of Wales)

John Evelyn (Wellcome)

Cosin's chapel at Auckland Castle

Black staircase in Durham Castle

Interior of Cosin's chapel at Auckland Castle (DCC)

Courtyard of Durham Castle (DCC)

HOSPITALE EPĪ DUNELM̄
PRO VIII PAUPERIBUS
FUNDAT̄ PER JOH̄ EPISCOP̄
A·D·MDCLXVI

Above the door of Cosin's Durham almshouse

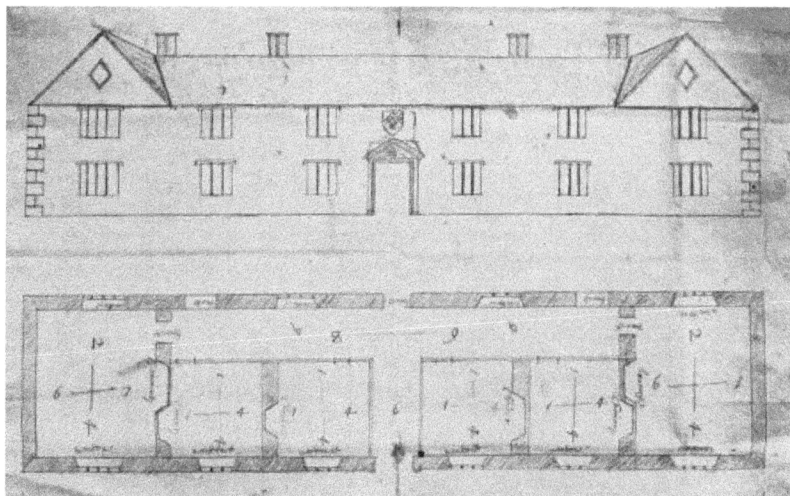

John Langstaff's design for Cosin's Durham almshouse

A 'tobacco drinker', 1623

Shakespeare's First Folio

Cosin's library on Palace Green, Durham
(Patricia Brown)

Cosin in later life

Trying to Keep Things Together

The exiled king's dream of regaining his throne with the help of the Scots came to an end at the battle of Worcester in September 1651. Outnumbered, outclassed and outwitted, Charles's exhausted, demoralised troops yielded to the superior strategy of Oliver Cromwell and his comrades, and the king was lucky to escape with his life. It was after the débâcle at Worcester that Charles experienced his famous adventures, adopting various disguises, and hiding in unlikely places such as an oak-tree, and several priest-holes. These had been designed to conceal Roman Catholic priests, in those days when they were liable to suffer dire punishments if caught. Stuffed into these tiny spaces, Charles was particularly uncomfortable because he had stopped growing at over six feet.

During his six weeks on the run Charles learned that some of his Roman Catholic subjects were loyal enough to risk their lives to help him. Hiding in a Catholic house with a Lancashire priest called John Huddleston, Charles discussed Catholicism, much as Cosin had discussed the Greek church with Archbishop Cyril. The fugitive king was shown the hidden chapel in the house, and looked over some Catholic books.

Although his height made him very conspicuous, and despite the fact that as many as sixty people were in on the secret, Charles was never betrayed, and he returned to Paris safely, though 'lean as Lent', dirty, unrecognisable to many, and without his luscious curls, in late October 1651. If anything, things had got worse for the royal exiles in the French capital. Money was very short, so that it looked like the English ambassador might have to move out of his house because of arrears of rent. The cash promised by the French royal family and others often failed to materialise, and at one point the king is said to have gone for ten days without eating any meat. The gift of a pack of hounds caused acute embarrassment as his majesty could not afford to feed them. When Charles dined with his mother at the Louvre, she kept a record of what he had eaten and drunk, in the hope that he would be able to pay her back when he was a little more flush. Relations between the two were not good – there was conflict between her group of exiles – called the Louvrains because of their residence at the Louvre – and those who took Charles's side.

At the time, the French were preoccupied with their own civil war, the so-called Fronde of the Princes, sparked by aristocratic discontent over the excessive power of the king and his chief minister, Cardinal Mazarin. The English king's attempt to intervene in this quarrel led to French resentment, making it dangerous for a while for the English courtiers to show their faces in the Paris streets. Mazarin, confronted by an apparently invincible republic across the Channel, negotiated a treaty with Cromwell's England. One result of this was that the cardinal offered Charles a steady income – but on condition that he leave France altogether within ten days.

As a royal chaplain, Cosin was keen to accompany the exiled king on his travels, but a letter from Charles revealed that his majesty wanted the dean to stay in Paris and continue his services at the ambassador's chapel, and as minister to the queen's Protestant courtiers 'to the end that no discountenance or discouragement, in these ill times, may dissolve that congregation'. Using the royal 'we', the king indicated that he was determined 'to use all possible means within our power for the maintenance and profession of that our religion in these times of slander, reproach, and persecution'. He added that 'we hope that God will so bless us, that we shall be able to reward the service you have done, and the sufferings you have undergone for us'.

While Charles and his entourage wandered from Spa to Aachen and then to Cologne, the 'sufferings' Cosin had 'undergone' in exile began to take a serious toll on his health. He sometimes fainted while officiating at services, and in October 1654 it was feared that he might not live to see Christmas. Poor and ill as he was, he still had to battle to keep his conception of the Church of England alive in exile. When Henry, Duke of Gloucester, a younger brother of King Charles, arrived in Paris in 1652, his mother Henrietta Maria set about trying to convert him to the Catholic faith.

Abbé Walter Montagu, the queen's confessor and almoner, was charged with drawing the young prince away from Anglicanism, and the queen herself assured young Henry that if he would only convert he could choose between the position of Roman Catholic cardinal of all England, or king in place of his Protestant brother Charles. Supposedly to protect Henry from the influence of dissipated persons in Paris itself, Montagu spirited the young man away to his abbey of St Martin at Pontoise, nearly twenty miles from the French capital.

Fighting back, Cosin asked Prince Henry's Protestant tutor, Richard Lovell, to 'read prayers out of the liturgy' to Henry in his bed-chamber, but Lovell refused on the grounds that this might offend Montagu. Cosin wrote out some arguments against Catholicism and in favour of Anglicanism that he thought Henry would do well to bear in mind during his discussions with Montagu: this paper was given to Griffith, a Protestant friend of the prince. The pair would look these over together at the dead of night. Meanwhile Henry's older brother King Charles warned him that if he *did* convert to Roman Catholicism, 'you must never think to see England or me again'.

The young duke's refusal to convert led his mother to cut him off without a penny. Charles ordered that Henry should be brought to him at Cologne, but it took the Duke of Ormonde, who was ordered to fetch him, two months to raise the money for the journey. Osmond is very harsh about Henrietta Maria's behaviour in relation to Henry at this time, calling her 'an unnatural mother, who little deserved so gracious a son', but when tempted to judge this unfortunate queen's conduct, it is as well to remember that by this time she had lost both a father and a husband to political violence, and that her life had been harsh in other ways as well. Today we are also less likely to accept without close scrutiny the opinions of men on the subject of what is and is not a 'natural' mother.

Cosin was involved in the fight to preserve the king's brother's loyalty to the Church of England: later he also involved himself in the task of supplying spiritual help to Lucy Walter, one of Charles's ex-mistresses. While Charles was forced to stay away from Paris, the beautiful Welsh courtesan made a full confession of her sins to Cosin. Although she may not have been Charles's first mistress (they got together when they were both eighteen) she is supposed to have given birth to the first of his many illegitimate children: James Scott, the first duke of Monmouth.

Later, Monmouth's political importance grew exponentially when it became apparent that Charles was not going to have any more children by his wife, the Portuguese princess Catherine of Braganza, who had suffered three miscarriages. The prejudice of the age meant that many resisted the succession of Charles's Roman Catholic brother, who became King James II. A wild story emerged that, during her confession to John Cosin, Lucy had revealed that she had in fact married Charles, and that their Protestant son James was therefore the legitimate heir to the English throne.

It was alleged that documentary evidence for Monmouth's legitimacy was kept by Cosin in a black box, which he was said to have passed on to his son-in-law just before his death in 1672. It was very bad luck for Monmouth that the fabled black box never did turn up. If it had, and the documents inside (if they ever existed) had been judged to be genuine, then the course of English history might have been quite different. The monarch called James II (if Monmouth had used that name as king) would have been Charles's son and not his brother, the rebellion that ended with Monmouth's execution in 1685 would have been quite unnecessary, and the so-called Glorious Revolution of 1688, when the real James II was deposed, would never have happened.

Charles would not have been judged to have married his Portuguese princess bigamously, however, since Lucy Walter died in Paris in September 1658, at the age of twenty-eight. In this alternative history, Charles would have been a widower when he married Catherine, and not a bachelor.

As well as his involvement in Prince Henry and Lucy Walter's lives, and his liturgical and administrative duties in relation to Anglicanism in exile, Cosin was called upon to write controversial literature at this time, despite his well-known poverty and ill-health. He wrote a book about the Holy Roman Empire, another about the Roman Catholics' supposed abuse of confession, and a third about transubstantiation – a key Catholic idea relating to the nature of the host eaten by Catholics as part of the Mass. Once again, the drift of Cosin's Latin treatise on transubstantiation was to assert that the ancient or primitive church, and the Anglicans, had got it right, while the 'Romanists' had 'stretched it with the absurdities of their opinion'. This little book was written in part to help King Charles in his disputes with Catholics on this vexed question.

As well as their different ideas about the nature of the host, the Anglican and Catholic churches of the time disagreed about which parts of the holy scriptures should be regarded as sacred and canonical. The Catholics had equal respect for the ancient books that many Protestant denominations had decided were apocryphal – these included the books of Judith, Ecclesiasticus and the first and second books of Maccabees. Cosin was required to write a book justifying the Church of England position on this matter: the result was his *Scholastical History of the Canon of Holy Scripture*.

Osmond attributed Cosin's eye problems at this time to the effects of his endless reading and writing, but excessive study is not usually listed among the causes of cataracts in modern medical sources. What may have caused the cataract in what Cosin called his 'reading eye' was his bad habit of smoking copious amounts of tobacco. In any case, this impairment was a source of immense frustration for Cosin, as it was now almost impossible for him to continue to read and write unaided. He wrote that 'not to be able to read (nor to write, but by guess, as now I do) is the greatest misery that ever yet befell me'. By writing 'by guess' Cosin presumably meant scratching away at the paper without really being able to see what he was writing. In this state, Cosin had to abandon his plan to write another book, on the validity of Anglican orders.

1660 and All That

By the time Charles II's ex-mistress Lucy Walter died in 1658, her relationship with the exiled king had been over, at least as far as he was concerned, for several years. In the meantime, she had not remained faithful to the man whom she is supposed to have claimed as her husband. In fact her behaviour and the claims she made were often scandalous, and, if it is true that she died young as a result of a sexually transmitted disease, then Cosin might have reflected that there was a kind of grim, heartbreaking inevitability about her fate.

Poor Lucy was not, however, the only person linked to the story of Charles's exiled court to die in 1658. In the same month and year, England's lord protector Oliver Cromwell died, at the age of fifty-nine. One can imagine the English exiles holding their breaths in anticipation of further developments, once the news had reached them.

Oliver was succeeded by his son Richard, who proved to be quite ineffectual and was soon ejected from power – as a result, he acquired the unfortunate nick-name 'Tumbledown Dick'. Into this power vacuum marched George Monck, a powerful, wealthy and sometimes ruthless old warhorse of a soldier, whom Parliament had allowed to become *de facto* military dictator of Scotland. On the second of January 1660, Monck led a force of eight thousand men south into England. By spring, parts of this Scottish army found themselves massed around London while Monck, from his position of great power, looked on as both houses of Parliament voted to invite Charles II back to his own kingdom. When the restored king landed at Dover on the twenty-fifth of May 1660, George Monck was the first person to embrace him.

It is not known whether Cosin found a place on a boat in the fleet of craft that returned Charles that May, but he was certainly in London by mid-June. Now well into his sixties and, as we know, suffering from poor eyesight, Cosin still found the time and energy to effect his own rapid restoration – to his rights in Durham, Peterborough and Cambridge. He also worked to restore his preferred style of divine services to Peterborough Cathedral, but his work in his old jobs had to be abandoned when he was made bishop of Durham.

There had been a proposal to make him dean of Durham, as he had been of Peterborough, but then his sufferings, loyalty and hard work in exile were remembered, and he found himself holding one of the most powerful posts available to a cleric in the Anglican Church. Although the position came with great wealth and unique powers and privileges, Cosin must have known, as he crossed the Tees for the first time as bishop in August 1661, that even if his sufferings in exile were over, there was still much hard work ahead of him, and not just in his diocese. Like 'the champion Conyers' who slew the Sockburn Worm, the new bishop had some serious challenges to face, and he would need more than an antiquated sword to tackle them.

During the Interregnum, bishops had been abolished in 1646, so that Cosin's predecessor at Durham, Thomas Morton, had been stripped of his status, his revenues and his residences. This was the Bishop Morton who had fled the diocese before the approach of the Scottish invaders in 1640. He had retreated to York in the first instance, and it is thought that he never returned to Durham. Later, in London, his coach was attacked by a mob, and from December 1641 he spent several months as a prisoner of Black Rod, a parliamentary official who still plays a prominent role in the pageantry of our state openings of Parliament. On his release, Morton retired to Durham House, the bishop of Durham's residence on the Strand in London; but in April 1645 he was imprisoned again, this time for six months, for refusing to hand over the seal of the county palatine of Durham, and for baptising an infant using the appropriate ceremony in the Book of Common Prayer. This celebrated prayer book and manual of Anglican belief and practice would later play a big part in the life of John Cosin.

In 1648 Morton was turned out of Durham House, and ended up doing the seventeenth-century equivalent of 'sofa-surfing' with friends, until he happened to meet one Christopher Yelverton on one of the roads into London. Yelverton asked him who he was, and, referring to the democratic process whereby bishops had been abolished, Morton replied, 'I am that old man, the bishop of Durham, in spite of all your votes.' Yelverton asked Morton to come and live with him at his house at Easton Maudit near Northampton, where the old bishop became a member of the family, and acted as tutor to his host's son. Morton died there in 1659, at the age of ninety-five. By a strange coincidence, the Christopher Yelverton who had offered him such hospitality was the son of Henry Yelverton, the judge who had tried to mediate between Peter Smart, and Cosin and his Durham associates.

The loss of its bishop was by no means the greatest tragedy to hit Durham during the Interregnum. In 1650, the year before Oliver Cromwell had won his victory at Worcester, he had inflicted a crushing defeat on the Scots at Dunbar. The upshot was that Cromwell ended up with perhaps five thousand prisoners on his hands, in Scotland, in September, in the middle of the perishing 'little ice age' of the seventeenth century. These men were led south on what can only be described as a death march to Durham, where three thousand were imprisoned in the cathedral: the English cathedrals were not used as places of worship at this time.

Allowing for the prisoners who were left in Newcastle, officers who had been separated out, and others who had managed to slip away en route, perhaps a thousand had died during the march south. A further seventeen hundred may have died in Durham itself, of cold, disease and malnutrition. Many of the Scottish dead were buried without any ceremony, and some were left above ground long enough for their bones to be gnawed by rats. We know this because in 2013 the bodies of a number of them were discovered under a disused courtyard among the university buildings on Palace Green.

The Dunbar prisoners are often blamed for the disappearance of much of Durham Cathedral's woodwork at this time: the story goes that they burned it as fuel. In my book *The Dunbar Martyrs* (2017) I suggest that much of the woodwork and many of the fittings may have been spirited away by Sir Arthur Haselrig, then the governor of Newcastle, and the man ultimately responsible for the fate of the Scottish prisoners. Haselrig, whose position also gave him a great deal of power south of the Tyne in County Durham, was well-known as an unprincipled and avaricious man. He was called 'a day-bed for the devil' and a 'church-thief', notorious for 'breaking up of sepulchres and searching the dormitories of the dead for hidden treasure, [and the sale of] the lead, iron bars, glass, pews, nay, pulpits'.

If Haselrig was indeed responsible for stripping much of the old woodwork out of Durham Cathedral, then this theft needs to be added to the vandalism he perpetrated at Auckland Castle, the home of the bishops of Durham. For a long time, many doubted the story that Haselrig had blown up the old chapel there with gunpowder, but recent excavations have revealed that that is exactly what he did.

Whether the Scots, Haselrig, the northern weather, neglect or a combination of factors was responsible, Durham Cathedral in 1660 had a leaky roof, broken windows, scorch-marks on the flagstones and broken and missing features both inside and out. Other buildings in the cathedral complex, and the bishop's castle on its mound across Palace Green, were also in a poor state, as was Auckland Castle.

To make the job of reconstruction even more difficult, many of the local church lands and other properties had been taken away from the church, so that at first there was little money coming in to finance repairs. Cosin, with his minute knowledge of the local church and its sources of revenue, combined with his sharp eye for detail, formidable administrative skill and tireless work-ethic, was the ideal man to claw back what he felt belonged to him and his associates. Cosin was allowed to be very successful in these efforts, even though Charles II's 1660 Declaration of Breda (of which more later) had seemed to promise that land bought during the Interregnum would not be wrested from its new owners.

As bishop of Durham, John Cosin was not only required to apply himself to the problems of his own diocese. Nationally, the deep divisions over religious matters that had long plagued the English had not magically disappeared when King Charles II had landed at Dover in May 1660. There were still plenty of Presbyterians and Puritans around, who harboured strong reservations about the new/old system of church government that had had the upper hand since the Restoration: a system which placed the monarch firmly at the top of the pyramid of the Church of England, with archbishops and bishops on the next step down. The objections many had to the new dispensation might hardly have mattered, had there not been a strong feeling at the top of the Anglican Church that there should be uniformity of worship and church organisation throughout the new Charles's kingdoms.

In the aforementioned Declaration of Breda King Charles had declared 'a liberty to tender consciences; and that no man shall be disquieted or called in question for differences of opinion in matter of religion, which do not disturb the peace of the kingdom'.

This seemed to promise dialogue between the different religious parties, perhaps with a view to cooperation and even unity. The possibility of bringing the Puritans and Presbyterians under the umbrella of the Church of England was explored at the Savoy Conference in London in 1661, at which John Cosin played a leading part. The ostensible purpose of the conference was to discuss the idea of revising the Anglican Book of Common Prayer in such a way that it would suit churchmen belonging to the opposing parties. The conference began on the fifteenth of April, after a short break necessitated by the coronation of Charles II, in which the new bishop of Durham was closely involved.

At the Savoy, twelve bishops, including Cosin, were ranged against twelve ministers of the Presbyterian variety (one of whom had by then become a bishop). The bishops who stood with Cosin were faced with opposite numbers who are by no means to be counted among the most radical would-be religious reformers of the age. There were no Baptists, Anabaptists or Quakers at the Savoy, for instance.

Prominent among the bishops' opponents was Richard Baxter, a powerful Puritan preacher and a prolific author. The discussion was destined to be a little lopsided, as it seems that the bishops on the opposite side were quite happy with the Prayer Book as it was, and had no changes to suggest. By contrast, the Presbyterians presented a list of so many changes that the bishops felt obliged to reject most of them.

Objections to the Book of Common Prayer raised by Puritans and Presbyterians were nothing new. In 1640 the so-called 'Root and Branch' petition, signed by fifteen thousand Londoners, had been presented to Parliament. The Petition stated that 'the liturgy for the most part is framed out of the Romish breviary, rituals, mass-book, also the book of ordination for archbishops and ministers framed out of the Roman pontifical' and also complained that 'the government of archbishops and lord bishops, deans, and archdeacons . . . have proved prejudicial and very dangerous both to the church and commonwealth'.

At the Savoy, the bishops on Cosin's side did concede some points to their opponents, but Osmond characterised their seventeen concessions as 'of slight consequence', and believed that Cosin had a hand in their rather sneering written answer to the would-be reformers' proposals. The reformers claimed 'that multitudes of sober pious persons' objected to the Prayer Book as it was: the conservative bishops countered that 'not only a multitude but the generality of the soberest and most loyal children of the Church of England' would object to such wholesale changes.

The proposed changes included the abolition of the Lent fast, an idea which the bishops characterised as 'contentious' and likely to split the Church of England off from 'the church catholic'. The reformers also wanted extempore prayer to be permitted, but the bishops doubted that any ability to make up prayers on the spot was really a gift of the spirit: after all it was something that 'any man of natural parts, having a voluble tongue and audacity, may attain to without any special gift'.

As well as the Lent fast, the reformers wanted to abolish saints' days and the reading aloud in church of passages from the Apocrypha. The bishops expressed similar objections to the reformers' proposals to ban the wearing of the surplice, the use of crosses, and members of the congregation kneeling to receive communion. In many cases, new ideas were objected to on the grounds that they would go against the practice of the ancient or primitive Christians.

The Savoy Conference looked destined to break up then and there without agreement, but John Cosin himself suggested a way of cutting through the verbiage: let the reformers make a list of everything in the Prayer Book that they regarded as 'contrary to the word of God'. The resulting eight-point list implied objections to the idea that all ministers had to subscribe to every word of the Prayer Book itself, that they had to use the sign of the cross during baptism, wear surplices, and force their parishioners to kneel when receiving communion, among other things.

As the time set aside for the conference began to run out, it was decided that Richard Baxter, and Peter Gunning, head of St John's College, Cambridge, should debate the sinfulness or otherwise of kneeling to receive communion. Unfortunately, both men were such aggressive debaters, Bishop Burnet wrote that the town 'thought here were a couple of fencers engaged in a thread of disputes, that could never be brought to an end, nor have any good effect'. It was all very diverting, but the conference broke up on July the twenty-fourth without having come to any agreement.

Richard Baxter's own account of the abortive conference is bitter in parts, and he accused John Cosin of speaking with 'little logic, natural or artificial,' so that no one was 'much moved by anything he said'. Baxter also found Cosin unfair and threatening, but mentioned his constant attendance at the conference, and also two other virtues that he perceived in the new bishop:

. . . one was, that he was excellently well versed in canons, councils, and fathers, which he remembered, when by citing of any passages we tried him. The other was, that as he was of a rustic wit and carriage, so he would endure more freedom of our discourse with him, and was more affable and familiar than the rest.

Reflecting on Baxter's second compliment to Cosin as printed above, Stranks, in his book *This Sumptuous Church*, expressed surprise that Cosin, a man born in the great city of Norwich, bred at Cambridge, and long exiled in Paris, could strike anyone as 'rustic'.

In some respects, the Savoy Conference of 1662 resembled the much earlier Synod of Whitby, which took place in 664 AD. That famous synod had a Durham connection: Cuthbert, the city's favourite saint, was in attendance. At Whitby, the issue was whether the then separate kingdom of Northumbria would embrace the Roman form of Christianity, or be a home for the Celtic variety. Whereas at the Savoy Conference the metaphorical battle-ground for much of the dispute was the future contents (or even existence) of the Book of Common Prayer, at Whitby there was much talk of the right way of calculating the correct date of Easter Sunday every year. The two conferences were different in that whereas there was a chance that certain compromises might have allowed unity between the two sides at the Savoy, Whitby was about picking a side between two parties that seem not to have been expected to reconcile.

Revising the Prayer Book

Although the 'fencing' divines at the Savoy Conference could come to no agreement over changes to the Book of Common Prayer, it was still felt that it needed some revision, and that John Cosin should be involved in the project. He had long been acknowledged as a liturgical expert, a safe pair of hands with an important ceremony (such as welcoming a doomed king into a cathedral) and he had after all written and compiled his *Collection of Private Devotions*, which was similar to the Book of Common Prayer in some respects. He was also acknowledged to be an excellent reviser and editor of existing texts. Cosin drew on his *Devotions* and his knowledge of older liturgies in English and other languages during his work on the Prayer Book.

The importance of the 1662 version of the Book of Common Prayer, to which Cosin contributed so many ideas, is hard to exaggerate. When Osmond was writing his biography of Cosin, on the eve of the Great War, something very close to the 1662 edition was still what we might call the 'manual' of Church of England practice. In twenty-first century England, the book has by no means been replaced. As its name should suggest, the Alternative Service Book (ASB) of 1980 was designed to offer alternatives to the ideas set out in the seventeenth-century Book of Common Prayer: the ASB was the forerunner of the Common Worship books which came into use twenty years later. Concern that the ASB was reducing the influence of the 1662 Book of Common Prayer led to the founding of the Prayer Book Society, 'established for the advancement of the Christian religion as set forth in the Book of Common Prayer'.

The language of this remarkable seventeenth-century book has worked its way into English culture in a way that only Shakespeare and the King James Bible can match. It is worthwhile to note that the King James Bible (1611), the First Folio of Shakespeare (1623) and the 1662 Prayer Book were all published within just over fifty years of each other, and all within John Cosin's life-time. A volume that was probably Cosin's personal copy of the First Folio, an early attempt to publish all of Shakespeare's plays in one volume, became famous when it was stolen from Durham in 1998.

As Brian Cummings points out in his 2011 edition of the Prayer Books of 1549, 1559 and 1662, phrases like 'in sickness and in health' (from the marriage service), and 'ashes to ashes, dust to dust' (from the burial service) are familiar even to English people who have never set foot inside an Anglican church. As well as marriage and burial, the 1662 Prayer Book sets out what its authors and editors wanted to enforce as the correct forms and wordings for baptism (both of babies and 'for those of riper years'), confirmation, 'thanksgiving for women after child-bearing' and 'the form and manner of ordaining bishops, priests and deacons'.

The book provides rituals to mark key life-events, and can also be used as a guide through 'the feasts and fasts throughout the year'; when they are supposed to happen and how they are to be marked. The section with 'tables and rules for the moveable, and immoveable feasts' begins with an explanation of the right way of calculating the date of Easter Sunday, which had been a major bone of contention between the Celtic and Roman churches in the days of St Cuthbert. This calculation had also been of great interest to Bede, Durham Cathedral's other great saint, who is buried in the Galilee chapel. Easter day, says the Book of Common Prayer, 'is always the first Sunday after the first full moon, which happens next after the one and twentieth day of March. And, if the full moon happens upon a Sunday, Easter day is the Sunday after'.

Turning to the end of the Prayer Book, readers will find the Thirty-Nine Articles, a sort of summary of Anglican theology, parts of which date from the short reign of King Edward VI (1547-53). Here they will also find the Table of Kindred and Affinity, derived from the Old Testament book of Leviticus, which advises men and women whom they may not marry. Women, for instance, may not marry their daughter's husband, or their daughter's daughter's husband.

The book also offers prayers to be said in times of drought, 'dearth and famine', bad weather, 'in the time of war and tumult' and 'in the time of any common plague or sickness'. There are also thanksgiving prayers for much-needed rain, 'fair weather' and 'for peace, and deliverance from our enemies'. Cosin himself is supposed to have re-cast a prayer of thanksgiving 'for restoring public peace at home', which may have had a special resonance early in the Restoration period.

A memorable instance of 'deliverance from our enemies' that happened when John Cosin was a small boy was the discovery of the Gunpowder Plot of 1605. The 1662 Book of Common Prayer included a church service to commemorate this day, when the congregation was supposed to give thanks 'for the wonderful and mighty deliverance' of King James I from 'popish treachery' which had made him, some members of his family, and Parliament, potential 'sheep to the slaughter'. Cosin himself was instructed to revise this service in 1662, which was altered again soon afterwards to incorporate thanks for England's deliverance from the Roman Catholic King James II. Osmond disliked this service, and rejoiced that 'since 1859 English churchmen have been spared the whole sorry performance'.

It is likely that Cosin had been sketching out ideas for a future possible revision of the Prayer Book for over thirty years. Among the treasures of his library on Palace Green in Durham is a large printed edition of the 1619 Prayer Book, covered in hand-written additions, many of them in Cosin's own hand, which is neat and legible even here, where he is making rough notes. Called the Durham Book, this much-annotated volume is a major source of evidence about what Cosin and his allies wanted to do with the Book of Common Prayer.

Not all of Cosin's suggestions for changes to the Prayer Book were accepted and incorporated in the 1662 edition. This is hardly surprising, since in theory any changes had to be approved by his own committee of revisers, a Church of England convocation, and both houses of Parliament, since the Prayer Book was part of English law, and not just a guide for English priests. An idea of Cosin's that seems to have been rejected, then accepted, was his suggestion that the practice of allowing services in Latin should be continued. This was something that had long been a custom at Oxford and Cambridge, and Latin translations of earlier versions of the Book had been published in 1551 and 1560. Jean Durel, the native of Jersey whom Cosin had presented for ordination in Paris, and who later became a canon of Durham Cathedral, published a Latin translation of the Prayer Book in 1670.

Other suggestions made by Cosin seemed to have the aim of forcing Anglican priests to apply themselves more rigorously to their liturgical duties. He wanted all parish priests to recite Matins and Evensong every day, unless illness or genuinely unavoidable absence prevented them. He also wanted Matins (quite reasonably) to take place in the morning, as early as six, and not 'when the morning is past, when . . . these services are commonly begun'. Perhaps because not everybody had Cosin's staunch work-ethic, these proposals were not adopted.

Various errors in the old Book of Common Prayer where corrected by Cosin, sometimes in collaboration with the aforementioned Bishop Matthew Wren. 'Annunciation of the Virgin Mary' became 'The Annunciation of our Lord to the Blessed Virgin Mary', which makes more sense, and obvious misprints were corrected. In some cases, the meanings of key words used in services had changed since the last revision of the Prayer Book, and had to be modernised. 'Till death us do part', in the marriage service, is Cosin's modernisation of the original 'till death us depart', which dated from a time when 'depart' could mean 'to separate'.

If Cosin had not substituted 'do part' for 'depart', brides and bridegrooms might have been confused by the wording of this particular vow for over three hundred years, thinking it meant something like 'until death departs from us'. Couples continue to be confused by the promise 'with my body I thee worship', which Osmond, who had evidently conducted his fair share of weddings using the Book of Common Prayer procedure, said provoked 'derision on the part of the ignorant, and in the minds of many it introduces an element of unreality at a very solemn moment'.

Many assume that this worshipping by the body has something to do with sex. The problem was evidently already a concern by 1655, when Anthony Sparrow, later bishop of Exeter, wrote his *Rationale upon the Book of Common Prayer*. Sparrow came close to apologising for the words, insisting 'and that no man quarrel at this harmless phrase, let him take notice, that to worship here signifies, to make worshipful or honourable'.

In support of his assertion of the harmlessness of the phrase, Sparrow quoted from an English translation of an old Jewish marriage service: 'be unto me a wife, and I according to the word of God, will worship, honour and maintain thee'. Although he no doubt understood that 'worship' here meant something like 'make honourable', Cosin still wanted to change the phrase to 'with my body I thee honour', but this was another of Cosin's ideas that was rejected.

Another of Cosin's rejected ideas relating to the marriage ceremony sheds a dim light on an obscure folk custom that the new bishop maintained was still prevalent 'in the north part of the kingdom'. As well as the familiar wedding ring, he wanted the bridegroom to be able to give his bride 'other tokens of spousage, as gold, silver, or bracelets'. It seems that this custom was not unique to the 'north part' of England. These shiny gifts, sometimes called *arrhae*, featured in some Spanish and French weddings, and were probably a vestige of the 'bride price' once paid by the groom or his family. *Arrhae* had once been provided for in English marriage services: Cosin would not have been introducing this option; merely re-introducing it.

The word 'congregation' was described by Cosin 'as a new word, never used by any former liturgy or ancient writer in the church'. He suggested that the phrase 'Church of Christ' could be substituted, as he was concerned that the use of the upstart word 'congregation' would play into the hands of the Church of England's Roman Catholic critics. Cosin succeeded in having many instances of 'congregation' removed from the 1662 Prayer Book.

Cosin and Wren also suggested psalms, new psalms or a choice of psalms to be read on certain holy days, such as Ash Wednesday and Good Friday. As regards the name of Sunday, for some the weekly holy day, Cosin proposed substituting 'the Lord's day', which would have been in keeping with the opinion of some Puritans, who pointed out that a day named after the sun is a pagan survival. The Quakers of the seventeenth century, whom Cosin persecuted, also refused to use 'Sunday', substituting 'first day'. Early Friends also eschewed the English names for all the other days of the week, and also the names of the months, some of which are derived from the names of pagan gods. The removal of the word 'Sunday' was another idea of Cosin's that was not adopted in the 1662 edition of the Prayer Book.

For the calendar of holy-days that was included in the 1662 edition, fuller descriptions of the days were copied from Cosin's earlier *Collection of Private Devotions*. New days were added, to mark the execution of King Charles I, and the feast-day of Durham's second favourite saint, Bede. St Alban, the first Christian martyr of the British, was given the incorrect date of June the seventeenth (it should have been June the twenty-second). Osmond regrets that Cosin seems not to have suggested the addition of St Cuthbert, whose tomb Charles I had visited during his visit to Durham Cathedral in 1633, or Oswald, the king and saint whose head is supposed to share Cuthbert's coffin.

In some of their suggestions for the Prayer Book, Cosin and Wren touched on ideas about the matters that had proved such bones of contention between Cosin and his old Durham critic Peter Smart. Cosin wanted chancels to be clearly separate from the rest of the church, and approved the use of screens to make the division clear. He also wanted to see special vestments worn by priests while celebrating the Eucharist, and to have them kneel or stand at certain points during certain services. Cosin's idea that the congregation should stand during the recital of a creed, and could even sing it, was accepted.

Smart had been particularly critical of where Cosin stood in relation to the altar when conducting the communion service: the instructions or 'rubric' on this subject in the 1662 Prayer Book are deliberately ambiguous. As Cosin wrote in his notes on these matters:

there was much ado about the posture of the table and the priests standing at it in King Edward's time . . . the priest was appointed to stand before the midst of the altar with his face towards it, and this was confirmed by Act of Parliament. Notwithstanding which Act, there were so many exceptions taken, and opposition made against that order . . . that at last they agreed to set forth this rule [north side].

As well as tinkering with these (to him very important) details, Cosin was able to add his own original writings to the 1662 edition, including an Advent prayer which Osmond singled out for particular praise, saying that it was 'instinct with a glowing but reverential affection'. The prayer makes more sense when we remember that new priests were often ordained during Advent:

ALMIGHTY God, our heavenly Father, who has purchased to thyself an universal Church by the precious blood of thy dear Son; Mercifully look upon the same, and at this time so guide and govern the minds of thy servants the Bishops and Pastors of thy flock, that they may lay hands suddenly on no man, but faithfully and wisely make choice of fit persons to serve in the sacred Ministry of thy Church: And to those which shall be ordained to any holy Function, give thy grace and heavenly benediction, that both by their life and doctrine they may set forth thy glory, and set forward the salvation of all men, through Jesus Christ our Lord. Amen.

Intolerance

To play a major part in the editing of a new edition of a prayer book may seem like an entirely harmless and positive thing to do, but in the paranoid atmosphere of the Restoration in England, the new Book of Common Prayer had the force of law, and it may not be going too far to say that it was weaponised. In the Advent prayer printed above, Cosin had proposed that congregations pray that the church 'may lay hands suddenly on no man, but faithfully and wisely make choice of fit persons'. Thanks in part to the new Book of Common Prayer, the authorities ejected some twelve hundred priests from the church, and laid violent hands on many who were now considered to be criminals because they could not agree to every word of the new Prayer Book.

The Prayer Book was prefaced by the Act of Uniformity, which insisted that any priest who was attached to the Church of England had to make a public declaration of his total support for every jot and tittle of the new edition. Failure to swear an oath to this effect in public by a set date would be punished by the priest's ejection from the Church of England, and therefore the loss of any income he drew therefrom. He would be stripped of all titles and positions in the church, and his legal status in relation to the church would be that of a dead man.

The draconian Act of Uniformity insisted not only on the declared fidelity of ordained priests to the new book. University professors, school-masters and even private tutors had to subscribe to the new liturgy, to declare that they held it 'not lawful upon any pretence to take arms against the king', and to agree that, whether or not they had personally sworn to the Presbyterian Covenant, the Covenant itself was 'an unlawful oath' and was no longer binding on anyone.

Teachers who persisted in teaching without having made this declaration could be put in prison for three months for a first offence. For subsequent offences, they could get three months and a fine of five pounds. In the 1660s, this sum was equivalent to over five hundred pounds today, and three months in a Restoration prison was a far more serious prospect than three months in a modern British jail. Especially for prisoners who could not or would not pay for their own upkeep inside, conditions could be deadly, and deaths from disease and starvation were common. The first Quaker known to have died for his beliefs, a teenager called James Parnell, died because the jailer at Colchester Castle forced him to sleep in a hole high up in a wall. Poor James was forced to climb up to and down from his hole, called 'the oven', to fetch his food. One day in 1655 Parnell fell down, and later died as a result of his injuries.

For priests like Richard Baxter, who had faced John Cosin and the other bishops across the table at the Savoy Conference, legislation and ejection were followed by outright persecution. He was no longer able to act as parish priest at Kidderminster in Worcestershire, where he had worked wonders through dedication, talent and deep religious conviction. With his new wife, Baxter moved from London to Acton – then a country village – in 1663. He continued to preach in his own house there, but by now the atmosphere had turned hostile for the so-called 'nonconformists' (the word had been around for some time, but now came into more general use). In March 1665 somebody fired a bullet into a house where Baxter was preaching. The projectile narrowly missed the head of his sister-in-law: nobody was hurt, but nobody could work out where the bullet had come from.

Eventually, Baxter ended up in prison because of his insistence on continuing to preach, even though his preaching was limited to his own house. Unlike many prisoners of the time, who starved in typhus-ridden hell-holes, Baxter found his first jail surprisingly pleasant. His jailer was kind and honest, his room large, and a pleasant garden was set aside for his exercise. The behaviour of his kind jailer contrasted with that of the notorious hanging judge, George Jeffreys, who tried Baxter in 1685, when the latter was seventy years old and in very poor health.

Baxter had recently published his *Paraphrase on the New Testament*, which was said to include attacks on the English religious establishment. Jeffreys took the opportunity of the preacher's appearance before him to swear at him, and insult him with terms such as 'old knave', 'old rogue', 'schismatical knave' and 'hypocritical villain'. In one of his rants against Baxter, Jeffreys revealed what may have been at the bottom of much of the religious persecution at the time: the paranoid fear of a religiously-inspired rebellion against the *status quo*, that it was feared might see a return to the old days of Oliver Cromwell's republic. 'It was notoriously known,' Jeffreys insisted, 'there had been a design to ruin the king and the nation. The old game had been renewed; and this person had been the main incendiary . . . don't let us be gulled twice in an age'. The upshot of Baxter's trial before judge Jeffreys was that the Puritan divine spent two years in prison.

When he was not locked up, Baxter still suffered harassment, and was often forced to move house. This was one reason why he could not get at his books (he seems to have been as much of a bibliophile as Cosin). These were housed in a rented room back in Kidderminster 'where they are eaten with worms and rats'. Meanwhile Cosin was able to build a library to house his own collection at Durham, and to employ people to catalogue it and take care of it.

Baxter was persecuted despite the fact that he continued to attend Church of England services, had tried to come to terms with the Arminians, and had once been considered so close to people like Cosin in his theological opinions that he had been offered a bishopric. After the Act of Uniformity of 1662 it was not only moderate Presbyterians like Baxter who suffered, however. Groups like the Quakers, who had only really been in existence for around a decade by 1662, were felt to be too extreme to ever reconcile with the state church, and suffered severe persecution, as we have seen in the tragic case of the first Quaker martyr, James Parnell.

Baxter himself counted the Quakers among the 'proper fanatics, looking too much to revelations within, instead of the holy scriptures'. He believed that he had prevented the Quaker plant from taking root back in Kidderminster – this he claimed to have done by inviting Quaker representatives to a debate, where he then proceeded to show up the supposed flaws in their arguments. Baxter also believed that the Quakers had been infiltrated by disguised Franciscan friars who used Friends' Meetings to spread their own brand of Roman Catholicism.

George Fox (1624-1691), the founder of the Quakers, was often in County Durham, which he called 'Bishopric' in his celebrated *Journal*. He wrote that in 1657 he visited Durham with the object of persuading 'a man come down from London' to abandon his plan of setting up England's third university in the city. Such learning, which the likes of Cosin rejoiced in, seems not to have been consistent with Fox's ideal of an inner, spiritual, plain form of religion. Fox believed that he had personally prevented the premature founding of Durham University, but in fact it was the death of Oliver Cromwell, the most powerful supporter of the scheme, which put paid to the idea.

Before the Restoration, local Quakers were relatively safe, as they found themselves under the protection of Judge Anthony Pearson, a convert to Quakerism, who lived at Ramshaw Hall near Durham. George Fox is known to have visited him there, and the Quaker founder claimed to have performed a miracle at Pearson's house. He met a woman there who could neither eat nor speak, 'and had been so a great while'. After Fox had spoken to her, 'she ate and spake and was well'.

Despite Pearson's efforts, some Durham Quakers did suffer persecution before 1660. In 1658 John, William and Thomas Richmond had valuable cattle confiscated, because of their refusal to pay tithes. In John's case, he lost forty pounds worth of cattle, though he only owed tithes to the value of eight pounds. In his *Journal*, George Fox mentions a visit to 'one Richmond's' in 'Bishopric'. It is likely that this Richmond lived at Heighington, where several Quakers with the surname Richmond lived at the time.

A Quaker called Margaret Ramsey was imprisoned at Durham 'for giving a godly exhortation to the people, after the priest had ended his sermon,' presumably in an Anglican church. The fact that they encouraged women to preach was one of the reasons why supporters of more traditional churches found the early Friends so disconcerting. In a tract published in 1680, George Hickes, then a London vicar, argued that the Quakers could not qualify as true prophets partly because they allowed women to speak, something that was forbidden by St Paul (see 1 Corinthians 14:34). It would be over three hundred years before the Anglican Church in England began to ordain female priests; in 1994.

The first Durham Quaker to die for his beliefs was George Humble, 'an aged man, who, seeing some of his friends put in the stocks, reproved the justice who had commanded it. The justice, offended at the reproof he deserved, sent the honest old man to jail for giving it, where, after about ten months confinement, he died'.

After the Restoration, when Cosin was bishop and Pearson returned to the Church of England, the 'sufferings' of the Durham Quakers, as they termed them, began in earnest. In 1660, numbers of Quaker men from Durham and Northumberland were locked up, some of them for months, in 'a nasty stinking dungeon' at Hexham. Later in the same year, Quakers from places like Lanchester, Wilton and Wall Nook were incarcerated at Durham, many because they had refused to take the Oath of Allegiance. About a hundred Friends were locked up there, many of whom had been arrested at their Meetings for Worship, the Quaker equivalents of church services. A letter published by Joseph Besse in his 1753 book *A Collection of the Sufferings of the People Called Quakers* reveals that because they had refused to pay 'a very avaricious and inhuman jailer' two shillings and sixpence a week each for their beds, twenty of them were thrown 'into a stinking dungeon, where we could not all lie down at once, where we remained five days'.

Also in 1660, four more Quaker men had goods of the value of three pounds and two shillings confiscated 'for absence from the national worship', meaning, of course, failure to attend Church of England services. In the summer of 1661, twenty-seven Quaker men and women were taken at a Meeting in South Shields and 'cast into nasty holes' at Tynemouth Castle, 'where they lay a full month'. Among them were 'yeomen', 'mariners', 'spinsters', merchants and 'Thomas Smith labourer'. Later in 1661, a Quaker called Thomas Williamson was fined five pounds for appearing in court with his hat on (Quakers refused to remove their hats out of respect, scornfully calling the practice 'hat honour'). Unable or unwilling to pay, Thomas was confined in the prison at Morpeth for three months.

The bishop of Durham himself is cited by Besse as the man responsible for fining one John Greenwell twelve pounds for attending Quaker Meetings. Cosin also confiscated four of John's cows, worth sixteen pounds altogether. As well as attending Meetings, local Quakers were fined and imprisoned for refusing to pay tithes. Some languished in jail for more than a decade, while the authorities took advantage of their absence in prison to confiscate their goods. In October 1665 Richard Errington and John Ushaw were sentenced to be transported to Barbados, but after waiting for nearly two years in 'close restraint' in Durham's House of Correction, Richard became ill and died. The House of Correction was only about thirty years old at this time: it had been built into one of the 'dry arches' under the west end of Elvet Bridge. A space that used to be part of the House of Correction is now the basement of a trendy bar.

In 1666 both male and female Quakers from the area were sentenced to transportation to either Barbados or Jamaica. In October of the same year, nine Friends were arrested 'by warrant from the bishop of Durham and other justices' at Meetings in private houses, six at Alnaby and three at Brancepeth. These were all sent to prison for two months, although one of those arrested, Constance Baker, was breast-feeding a baby at the time. In 1663, George Fox had been alerted to the possible consequences of Church of England priests taking up their duties as local justices. He knew that many Durham priests had done this, and an unnamed Friend warned him that if they could get hold of Fox, they would tie him to a stake and burn him.

As well as ordering raids on Quaker Meetings, Bishop Cosin was also responsible for employing the local militia or 'trained bands' to take twelve Quaker men from their own homes and drag them before one Justice Tempest, who had them all locked up. Cosin was not the only cleric who was responsible for having local Quakers incarcerated. In 1668 Thomas Davison, vicar of Norton, made sure that one Simon Townsend was imprisoned for seven years, for refusal to pay tithes.

Sometimes the glaring injustice of the harsh sentences meted out to local Quakers turned the stomachs of the men employed to impose them. When, in 1670, Thomas Pyborne was fined six pounds and six shillings just for attending Quaker Meetings, Miles Gerry, the constable who was supposed to extract the fine, refused to do so. As a result Gerry's own goods were taken away, to the value of the fine, and Pyborne ended up paying six pounds and six shillings to the conscientious constable. John Brown, the constable of Coundon, also refused to extract seven pounds from his Quaker neighbour John Langstaff, and ended up losing some of his own property as a result.

Thomas Dawson of Norton kept some 'brass utensils' that had been confiscated (or 'distressed') from a Quaker, in his own house for over a year; but when he lay on his death-bed he evidently felt that this brass-ware was tainted, and comprised ill-gotten gains, and insisted that it be removed from his home.

Also in 1670 Thomas Davison, the aforementioned vicar of Norton, who had had Simon Townsend sent away for seven years, refused to punish an unnamed 'Quaker's wife', although she had illegally cut down some trees in the county to which Bishop Cosin felt he had a claim. This was despite the fact that Davison's parish 'hath so many obstinate men and women . . . that will not yet lay down their conventicles [meaning illegal religious assemblies]'. We know about Davison's problems and decisions at this time thanks to some letters written by Cosin. In one of them, the bishop writes approvingly of how in London the 'meeters' 'are ferreted out of every hole by the train-bands of the city' and how the troopers 'will watch them hereafter at all hours'.

Cosin was evidently concerned to keep a similar watch on his local recusants, or Roman Catholics who refused to attend Church of England services. In May 1670 he wrote to one of his assistants asking for a list of all the convicted female recusants in the city of Durham, together with their addresses, 'as Silver Street, Market Place, Crossgate, and the Old Baileys [no doubt meaning what we now call North and South Bailey]'.

Ornsby writes that although Cosin may have been 'not indisposed to treat the non-conforming ministers with some degree of lenity and forbearance' he still acted against them with 'sufficient rigour'. Likewise 'popish recusants . . . gave him no little trouble'. Ornsby adds that 'the Church of Rome had still a large number of adherents in the northern counties, some clustering around the halls of such of the gentry as still clung to the ancient faith, others scattered up and down the sequestered dales of the rural districts'. A 1662 letter to Cosin from Gilbert Sheldon, the bishop of London, hints that Sheldon himself had had to defend Cosin's 'severity' against his local recusants and thus 'stop the mouths of some great ones'. 'If you have done no more than what you write,' Sheldon adds, 'you could not do less, and having those provocations in Northumberland, 'twas much you did no more'. In his letter, Cosin's correspondent remarked that 'the recusants are . . . like the Presbyterians, who cry out, "persecution, persecution," unless they may do and say what they list'. Anglicans like Cosin and Sheldon may have thought of themselves as moderates, treading a quiet, dignified middle way between the noisy extremes of Roman Catholicism and Presbyterianism.

John Langstaff

An honest symbolic painting of John Cosin as bishop of Durham might depict him with one hand open, dispensing charity, and the other holding a stick to beat members of groups like the recusants and the Quakers. In the style of many medieval depictions of the founders of churches and other worthy institutions, the bishop might also be shown with models of his almshouses, his library on Palace Green in Durham, and his chapel at Auckland. If there was room somewhere in the painting, it might also be possible to squeeze in one or more of the books he wrote, or to which he contributed.

The charitable and persecuting aspects of Cosin's time as bishop came together rather uncomfortably with his ambitious building schemes in his relationship with John Langstaff, the Quaker mentioned near the end of the last chapter, whom the Coundon constable, John Brown, refused to fine.

Langstaff was a wealthy building contractor, living in a house that was sometimes described as a 'mansion', at Bishop Auckland. He is supposed to have been converted to Quakerism (or, as the Quakers would say, 'convinced') at Ramshaw Hall, the house of the aforementioned Quaker judge, Anthony Pearson, in 1653. It is said that James Nayler, whose importance as a Quaker leader almost matched that of the slightly younger George Fox, was also present under Pearson's roof at the time. Nayler, whose actions later alienated many Quakers, suffered dire punishment in London in 1656. There he was publicly whipped, and branded on the forehead, and his tongue pierced with a hot poker.

In 1653, John Langstaff was caught up in a colourful incident at Auckland involving Anne Audland, a Quaker preacher from Kendal (now in Cumbria). Anne was locked up in the town jail for preaching the Quaker gospel, but managed to continue preaching to the locals out of the window of her cell. John Langstaff was so inspired by her words that, when she was released, he took her home. Perhaps because Anne was a young woman in her twenties, Langstaff's wife was not happy about the visitor, and the girl from Kendal felt obliged to leave, and seek a field to sleep in. But she was rescued by our friend Anthony Pearson, who took her home to Ramshaw Hall.

1653 is supposed to be the date when proper Quaker Meetings began to be held in County Durham. This was also the year when Quaker Monthly Meetings (now called Area Meetings) were first held in Durham City. These are Meetings where matters to do with the business, administration and finances of a group of local Quaker Meetings are discussed. From the start, John Langstaff seems to have been regarded as an important and trustworthy Friend: what Quakers call a 'weighty Friend'. He was entrusted with the Monthly Meeting finances, perhaps because he was known to be good with money and was too rich to be tempted to abscond with the kitty.

Although he was evidently a very practical man, a mason by training who had built up an impressive business, John Langstaff's spiritual side asserted itself one night in 1662, when 'he was stirred up in the night by the spirit' and sat down to write a strange letter to the local justices, full of prophecies and warnings of 'many strange judgements' that he felt 'do hang over this kingdom and government'. As a result of drawing attention to himself and his Quaker beliefs in this way, Langstaff was sentenced to praemunire, a nasty legal tactic from medieval times that had been revived for use against the Quakers and other sectaries, whereby the victim's entire estate, together with his freedom, could be taken away.

In August and September 1670 John was fined ten shillings a week for four weeks in a row for attending Meetings at Heighington, which probably did not bother him as much as the fine of eleven pounds he had to pay in the same year, because of his refusal to pay tithes. The records of the archdeacon of Durham reveal that in 1673 John Langstaff was in trouble again, this time for keeping his children unbaptised (Quakers do not baptise either infants or those 'of riper years'). Besse also records the fact that Langstaff was fined twice in 1678 for attending Meetings at Stockton, Norton and Raby.

Meetings for Worship were regularly held in two houses belonging to John Langstaff, and in the winter of 1666 three male Quakers were sentenced to seven years' transportation for attending such Meetings, probably at John's Auckland 'mansion'.

By the time the Langstaff surname came down to George Blundell Longstaff its first 'a' had become an 'o'. In his 1923 book *The Langstaffs of Teesdale and Weardale* George suggested that the reason why his ancestor may not have been transported like the other Quakers who had met at his house in 1666 was that Bishop John Cosin needed Langstaff's expertise as a builder, and could not spare him. Longstaff points out that after Cosin's death his ancestor *was* imprisoned, though not transported, in 1672 and 1677.

In a short but well-judged study of Cosin published in 1978, C.J. Stranks reminded his readers that, given his secular powers and responsibilities in the county, the bishop was obliged to persecute Quakers and other non-Anglican groups. This is certainly the case, but if Cosin personally found the Quakers distasteful and even alarming, it is hardly surprising. Their numbers had grown rapidly since around the middle of the century, and people of all types and classes had been 'convinced'. According to Fox's *Journal*, their number even included an unnamed 'Common-Prayer-Man', who had presumably stood out for the old Prayer Book against the innovations of the Puritans during the Interregnum. As a man who advocated elaborate church ritual, furnishings and architecture, Cosin may have felt a natural distaste for the Quakers' apparent total lack of any of these. Cosin's love of books and learning is perhaps his most attractive feature: George Fox's suspicion of advanced learning in particular can seem boorish in the modern context.

We know about Cosin's working relationship with John Langstaff, the Quaker contractor of Bishop Auckland, from the bishop's surviving letters, and documents such as accounts and contracts. Langstaff worked on Cosin's library and almshouse on Palace Green in the city of Durham, on buildings in the Auckland Castle complex, on the bishop's manor house at Darlington, and on an estate Cosin had bought at Brafferton in North Yorkshire.

It seems that Langstaff already had a reputation as a builder to the rich and powerful before the Restoration: he was credited (if that is the word) with the demolition of the old chapel at Auckland Castle, when the place was owned by Arthur Haselrig. After the Restoration, Cosin employed Langstaff to help build a new chapel based on what had been the great hall of the castle, among other things, and to re-use parts of Haselrig's new buildings that Cosin wanted demolished. The surviving contracts and accounts reveal that Langstaff was also paid separately for specific jobs such as clearing away rubble, delivering loads of building materials such as lead and slates, making bricks, and perhaps even brewing and supplying beer; although George Blundell Longstaff believed that John Langstaff the brewer was a different man.

It is not impossible that John Langstaff the Quaker contractor of Bishop Auckland owned a brewery and contracted to supply beer, to the bishop and others. That he was not frightened of going beyond his own training and expertise in order to make money is shown by the fact that he attempted to persuade Cosin to lease him some of his land so that he, Langstaff, could sink and run coal mines under the land itself. By Cosin's time, Durham had already been famous for its reserves of high-quality coal for some centuries, but the bishop turned down Langstaff's offer on legal grounds, and because he thought that even if the resulting mines were only worked for a short time, the inconvenience of having mines, miners, coal-wagons and the miners' 'hovels or houses' on his land might be resented by future bishops of Durham.

Another investment Langstaff wanted to become involved in was closer to his core business as a building contractor, and his training as a mason, than either coal-mining or the brewing of beer. To judge from a November 1671 letter of Cosin's, Langstaff wanted to rent 'the freestone quarry at Coundon' from the bishop, but Cosin was unsure whether in was already being rented out to somebody else, and in any case wanted to keep Langstaff out of it because he was unsatisfied with his work at Brafferton: 'If John Langstaff had done anything for me at Brafferton I should have been more willing to let him have his request'.

The bishop's letters that mention Langstaff are often written from London, from which distant city Cosin was endeavouring to oversee the details of Langstaff's work in Durham and Yorkshire. Not surprisingly, the tone of some of these letters is sometimes distinctly tetchy. Cosin complains that he cannot understand parts of the letters and drawings sent to him, and is clearly frustrated that he has to rely on other people's sometimes vague, incomplete, tardy and irrelevant written accounts in order to build up a picture of what is going on. Where there are disagreements or problems (for instance a leaky roof in the library) the solution Cosin often insists on is the rapid deployment of John Langstaff who, Cosin seemed to think, was capable of sorting everything out as long as he was carefully instructed and then narrowly watched.

Here and there in the letters there are hints that Cosin's correspondents in the north may have been tempted to employ a cheaper contractor: when the front of a house had to be re-faced, the bishop insisted that 'no patcher' be employed, 'but that John Langstaff should set on neat workmen to do it'. The terms 'neat' and 'artificial' are often employed by the bishop when writing about buildings and building-work. In his day 'artificial' meant something like 'well made', as it did in Shakespeare's time; it did not mean 'fake' as it does today.

It may be that Langstaff's status as the best local builder explains why Cosin was determined to use him on projects in Durham City when he was actually based at Bishop Auckland. In theory, all the Durham jobs should have gone to masons and other builders based in the city. There is evidence to suggest that the guilds of the time were aware of this affront to the usual arrangements: it is yet another example of the power wielded by the prince bishops of Durham.

The detail Cosin goes into in some of his letters regarding his building projects is astounding, and may hint at something of an obsessive nature. Certainly one feels that the bishop's agents in the north cannot always have looked forward to his letters with gleeful anticipation. Addressing the matter of Langstaff's workmen building 'the additional library at Brafferton' in 1670 the bishop expressed his concern that if the carpenters worked 'at the bottom of the great staircase' their candles might set light to the inevitable wood-shavings and start a fire. He insisted that the workmen be moved to 'the great hall, by the fire-side, or rather in the great kitchen'.

There are hints in the letters that Cosin thought that he was being hoodwinked by some of his correspondents, whom he may have suspected of trying to skim off a proportion of the vast sums he was spending on demolition, repairs, refurbishment, decoration and construction. Why were sixteen trees cut down at Bedbourne in 1670 when only six were needed to repair the nearby mill? Were the trees sold or given? If they were sold, who paid for them? When I asked you how high the new wall of the library now was, why did you dodge the question and merely tell me that Langstaff is building it 'as fast as he can'? Did you think I didn't know that Langstaff was behind the scheme to sink coal-mines into my land?

When you wrote to me about the new room Langstaff has added to the library (on Palace Green), why did you make your account 'so hard and obscure that it is not possible for me to understand it'? Were you trying to cover up the fact that Langstaff has not yet knocked through the new door between the two parts of the library, although I have repeated my instructions about that door more than once? 'If this be not done, nothing is done, for I understand not a syllable of what you write concerning two doors in the new room'. If the new door has been knocked through, what have you done with the presses (meaning book-cases) that stood where I want the new door to go? Can't you get Langstaff to make 'a little draught [meaning drawing] and description of it on a piece of paper'?

Much of the correspondence concerning Langstaff's work on the new library reveals Cosin's concern for the welfare of his precious books. He does not want Langstaff's workmen tramping through his library on their way to and from work, so he toys with the idea of having a temporary access door installed. When the roof springs a leak, he is naturally concerned that the books will get wet, and when winter comes on he wants all of his books and other possessions carefully examined for mould and other damage. He asserts that 'moulding' can be prevented by having his books 'all rubbed over before a fire once a fortnight or month at least' during the winter.

Cosin wanted the books in his Palace Green library to be well looked-after: he also wanted them to be presented to the world in a sumptuous and attractive manner. To this end he paid for the artist Jan Baptist van Eerssell to paint portraits of various worthies in the spaces above the book-cases. Van Eerssell also did work at Auckland Castle. A December 1668 letter penned by Cosin reveals that although 'everybody that comes to me from Durham speaks highly of the library-room' at first they found van Eerssell's pictures 'very ugly and unworthy of the room: he hath need therefore to go over the faces again and mend them that they may not look like Saracens, as all comers say they do'.

Cosin ordered a catalogue of the Palace Green collection to be drawn up. This work was entrusted to the bishop's son-in-law, Thomas Blakiston, the second husband of his daughter Frances. Thomas was descended from a distinguished Gibside family, but it seems that this did not fit him for the task of drawing up a library catalogue. Ornsby states that Thomas was 'obviously a careless, indolent man, and under his hand the catalogue is said never to have advanced beyond the letter D'. In his book on Cosin, C.J. Stranks suggested that, despite the frustrations associated with the project, his library on Palace Green was the old bishop's pride, joy and consolation in his last years. If he had felt able to retire like a modern bishop, Cosin might have enjoyed completing his catalogue himself, as a worthwhile retirement project, during his autumn days.

Although its compilation was proceeding so slowly, Blakiston's catalogue revealed gaps in the collection that Cosin worked hard to fill up. One can imagine himself or his agents scouring the London book-shops for rare manuscripts and printed books to make the collection more complete. People who owed the diocese money for one reason or other were encouraged to contribute a book to the library in lieu of payment. In a letter of October 1670, Cosin writes that he will be content with the fine offered in relation to two Durham water mills, unless his correspondent 'can hook in a book'. Book collectors were also encouraged to contribute volumes on the grounds that they would be better looked after in Cosin's library than they might be elsewhere (always assuming that they were robust enough to survive being rubbed all over in front of a fire once a fortnight during the winter).

Perhaps the most famous book in Cosin's collection is the aforementioned First Folio of Shakespeare. Like Leornardo's painting of the Mona Lisa, which was stolen from the Louvre in 1911, the Durham First Folio became famous when it was taken without the owners' consent. As we have seen, this happened in 1998: other printed books, and some manuscripts dating from the fourteenth and fifteenth centuries, were stolen at the same time. Altogether, the haul was worth over fifteen million pounds.

The Durham First Folio reappeared in 2008 when a local man called Raymond Scott tried to sell it to the prestigious Folger Shakespeare Library in Washington D.C. The experts at the Folger quickly identified it as the missing Durham copy, and Scott was subsequently locked up. The other items that were stolen from Durham have never reappeared. As manuscripts, some of these were unique, unlike Shakespeare's First Folio. Perhaps a thousand copies of this book were printed in 1623, of which two hundred and thirty-five are known to have survived. It is quite possible that John Cosin bought his copy new, for just one pound. A number of Shakespeare's plays had been published before the First Folio, but around eighteen of them appeared for the first time in print in 1623. This means that if the First Folio had never been published, we might never have known plays like *Twelfth Night*, *The Tempest* and *Macbeth*.

The Durham First Folio had been mutilated by the time it reached the Folger in 2008, reducing its value from around three million pounds to about half of that amount. Somebody, perhaps Scott, had removed the cover, which showed that the book had once been in the library of Peterhouse College, Cambridge, where Cosin had been master. It was evidently one of the books Cosin was able to have transferred from Cambridge to Durham. As we know, other books, many of them in French, were transferred from Paris at the Restoration; and Cosin added more books to his library when he was bishop of Durham. The Durham First Folio came home to Palace Green in 2010. It is supposed to be the only copy of the Folio which has been in the same collection or library since the early seventeenth century. Apart from its time in the company of thieves, it has never changed hands.

Other notable books Cosin owned, and are still kept in his library at Durham, include a 1516 first edition of *Utopia* by Thomas More, complete with sixteenth-century calfskin binding: this is another book that Cosin may have acquired in Paris. Cosin also owned a copy of Francis Bacon's *Essays* with a luxurious velvet cover, featuring an embroidered portrait of King Charles I's favourite, the aforementioned George Villiers, first duke of Buckingham. This may have been given to Cosin by the ill-fated king himself.

Today Cosin's library is a grade one listed building, and its collection, with its many unique volumes, is considered to be of international importance. It may not be too whimsical to say that walking into this extraordinary space is like walking into Cosin's own mind: well-stocked, orderly but perhaps a little gloomy. Van Eerssell's portraits of high-brow worthies, including Plato, Aristotle and Plutarch, provide distinguished company for the lonely scholar privileged to study here. It is no surprise that one of them depicts Jacobus Arminius, the Dutch theologian whose name was given to the type of theology that Cosin embraced.

Around Palace Green

Cosin's library on Palace Green in Durham is supposed to have been built on the site of some old stables or outhouses belonging to Durham Castle. This is hardly surprising, since visitors taking a clockwise route round Palace Green will come across the entrance to the castle shortly after they pass the library. John Cosin was the last of the prince bishops to make major changes to the castle, parts of which date from Norman times.

Cosin filled in the moat and landscaped the mound on which the ancient keep still stands, making room for gardens, driveways and terraces. He also installed an ornate porch around the entrance to the great hall, reinforced various other structures, and installed a new water supply. Cosin's panelling in the great hall is no longer in place, but his efforts to refurbish Bishop Tunstal's fifteenth-century chapel are still evident.

By far Cosin's most impressive surviving addition to the castle complex is his so-called black staircase. This is enclosed in its own stair-tower, and was supposed to be a cantilevered or 'flying' staircase. Unfortunately it began to sag soon after construction, and massive vertical wooden beams had to be inserted. It is still possible to see these and the sagging that they arrested. The overall effect of Cosin's improvements to the castle were to make the place less of a defensive, military building and more like a fine city dwelling. The place was taken over by Durham University in 1837 and now serves as a college and hall of residence.

As we have seen in the case of the bishop's possible fourteenth-century ancestor John Cosyn of Norwich, before the Reformation, wealthy and distinguished English people could pay to set up chantries, where prayers would be chanted for the welfare of their eternal souls in perpetuity, or until the building fell down, the money ran out or the the Reformation came along. In the new Protestant atmosphere that followed Henry VIII's Reformation, people concerned about the fate of their souls in the afterlife had to find other ways to be remembered, and perhaps prayed for, after death.

Although Cosin's various building projects in his bishopric certainly had charitable and educational value, and added to the dignity of future bishops of Durham and to the Church of England in general, Cosin did not hesitate to 'label' these places with his coat of arms, or cause inscriptions to be carved onto them that mentioned him by name.

A coat of arms, carved in relief and coloured, stands over such an inscription above the main door of Cosin's almshouse on Palace Green in Durham. Like the library that it faces across the Green, this was built by John Langstaff, and Langstaff's 'draughts' or sketches of the structure are still extant. As the recently-refurbished inscription over the door states (in Latin) the almshouse or 'hospital' was intended to be home for eight 'paupers'. This is evident from the front elevation, the central part of which has eight windows facing the Green. The central section is flanked by two matching structures which Cosin had built to re-house a grammar school and music school respectively. These schools had been founded by Cosin's predecessor Bishop Langley in 1414, and Cosin's almshouse was built on their original site.

Although John Langstaff built Cosin's Durham almshouse, he could not have lived in it unless he had abandoned his Quakerism. This he seems never to have done: although James Raine, in his book on Auckland Castle, suggested that the Quaker builder defected back to the Church of England, there is evidence that Langstaff was an active Quaker until his death in 1694. The almshouse was designed for four Anglican men and four women who were either spinsters, bachelors, widows or widowers. The inmates had to be over fifty-five, and three of each sex had to be from Durham: the other two could be from Brancepeth. They were hand-picked by the bishop (or the dean and chapter of the cathedral if there was no bishop), and were expected to march off to worship at the great church every day, unless they were too sick to do so. They were to wear their distinctive gowns to church, something that would have reminded anyone who saw them that Cosin had paid to house them, feed them and clothe them. He had also endowed the almshouse in such a way that a nurse would always be available.

The occupants of Cosin's almshouse in Durham were expected to behave themselves, to live soberly and humbly, to refrain from taverns and bad company, and to sleep every night in the almshouse. Repeated failure to live up to these standards could be punished by ejection. Presumably any of the oldsters who took it into their heads to marry or re-marry in later life could also be kicked out. Writing about the institution in his 1872 book *History of the Charities of the City of Durham*, C.M. Carlton noted that the value of the monies allotted to the almshouse by Cosin had diminished considerably in the one hundred and seventy years since its foundation, leaving the place and its occupants in dire financial straits. By Carlton's time the beneficiaries of Cosin's charity had been moved into new premises in nearby Queen Street (now Owengate) which had been built by Bishop Maltby. Cosin's almshouse near his other castle at Bishop Auckland was re-built by Maltby in 1845.

Cosin's almshouse on Palace Green was taken over by Durham University in 1837, and served as student accommodation until it became the university museum in 1876. It housed some of the university's collection of stuffed birds, which had been suffering from the damp of their previous home, the old Fulling Mill by the River Wear. The Fulling Mill Museum was closed in 2012 partly because of the damp conditions by the river, which were made worse by snow, ice and flooding. By that time, the university was opening up alternative exhibition spaces on Palace Green.

When Cosin's almshouse was one of the university's museums, its ornithological exhibits included a stuffed great auk; a flightless north-Atlantic sea-bird that became extinct around 1850. Also on show were some personal effects that had once belonged to 'Count' Joseph Boruwlaski, a little person from Poland who died in Durham in 1837, at the age of ninety-seven. Some of the items that once belonged to the Little Count can still be seen in the old Durham town hall on the Market Place (see my *In Search of the Little Count*, 2008).

To convert the almshouse into a museum, the university removed many of the internal walls, and the floor that divided the ground floor from the first floor, creating two large rooms with high ceilings, one on each side of the ornate central door. The building is now a café: customer seating is in the left-hand room; the kitchen and serving area are to the right.

Some of the rich of seventeenth-century England undoubtedly tried to outdo each other with the magnificence of their houses, parks and carriages, and the generosity of their provision for the poor. Since these institutions could continue to bear their donors' names for centuries, almshouses were a good way to give, and to be seen to be still giving, even after death. One of the wealthiest men in Durham towards the end of Cosin's life was John Duck, sometimes called the Butcher Baronet or Durham's Dick Whittington.

Duck made his fortune buying and selling cattle, and in 1670 he was in dispute with Cosin over some stolen cattle that he, Duck, had bought cheap at only two pounds per beast. That is about the sum of what we know about the case, but it could have caused enduring bad blood between the two men. Duck's founding of his own almshouse at Great Lumley in 1686 may have been an attempt to outdo the old bishop, who by that time had been dead for fourteen years. Duck's almshouse looked similar to Cosin's Durham institution, but housed twelve inmates instead of Cosin's eight. To judge from old photographs, the main staircase inside Duck's palatial house on Silver Street in Durham may also have been intended as a miniature version of Cosin's celebrated black staircase in the Durham Castle complex.

Duck's career is comparable to that of John Langstaff, the Quaker contractor of Bishop Auckland, except that, like Cosin and unlike Langstaff, John Duck was a loyal high-church Anglican. He rented a pew in St Nicholas's church in the Market Place, and donated church decorations. He and his wife were both buried under a broad carved stone set in the floor of St Margaret's church on Crossgate in Durham.

Still moving clockwise round Palace Green, we come to the cathedral, over which, as the local bishop, Cosin exercised considerable influence. Much of his power over the ancient church lay in his duty to carry out visitations of the cathedral every three years. These might be likened to modern external inspections of schools, external audits of company accounts, and the annual appraisals endured by employees of many modern organisations. In theory, cathedral officials who were diligent and honest had nothing to fear from the bishop's detailed probing, but for them Cosin must still have seemed like a formidable inquirer, with his eye for detail and his prior knowledge of how this particular cathedral worked.

Cosin's visitation articles (really a numbered list of searching questions) survive from his second visitation of the cathedral, in 1665. They include basic, general questions designed, for instance, to check that the cathedral had its full complement of staff, that they were all paid properly, and had been admitted to their jobs in the proper way. The articles then inquire into the general behaviour of these employees: 'are they all of good fame and honest conversation [meaning general behaviour]?' Do they actually turn up to perform their duties, or are they frequently absent without good cause? 'Are they known, famed, or suspected, to live in any grievous or scandalous crime, or have they committed any other offence that is punishable by ecclesiastical censures?'

Although some of the articles of visitation are derived from earlier models not written by Cosin himself, the bishop's particular interests are reflected in some of them: 'is the Book of Common Prayer . . . duly observed in all things without alteration or omission?' Cosin also inquires about the cathedral library, asking if the sacrist '(or some other appointed by the Dean and Chapter) diligently look to the common library of the church, and see that the books be well-bound and preserved there?' He also asks after 'any books that have been in the late wicked and distempered times embezzled and taken away, either by violence or fraud, and in whose hands they now are?' Is there a proper catalogue or 'register'? When books are issued, is a proper record kept of who took them and when?

In his thirteenth article, Cosin refers to what we now call the Interregnum as 'the late violent and impious and rebellious times', thus avoiding repetition of the words 'wicked and distempered'. Like several of the visitation articles of 1665, and the fragmentary responses to them that have survived, Cosin's article thirteen provides evidence of the ruinous state of the cathedral complex, even five years after the Restoration. The bishop asks after floors, walls, roofs, woodwork and windows: are they being repaired or replaced in an appropriately 'fair' and 'orderly' manner 'without patching' or the introduction of 'ruder work'? Is the result that after restoration things are 'made, if not better, at least not worse, than they were of old?'

In answer to Cosin's inquiries concerning the church's fabric, the dean and prebendaries of Durham insisted that they had done as much as they could in so short a time to restore their cathedral. 'We can truly say,' they wrote, 'that the inhabitants of this city, neighbours, and strangers (especially those who had seen the ruins before) that occasionally resort hither, wonder to see how much we have done in so few years, and how well we have done it'.

At first, they explain, they had hired a large number of workmen, who laboured under a master-workman who was paid a stipend of forty pounds a year. Reading between the lines, it would appear that, looking around at the cathedral complex, these men realised that if they spun the work out, they would have jobs for life, and so they proceeded slowly. Soon, however, the cathedral hierarchy realised what was happening (or not happening) and so they began to hire men to perform specific tasks for specific amounts of money, the work to be completed within a specified time-frame. 'By which means,' the dean and prebends assert, 'they have done more in four years than would have been done in seven, if we had gone on as we began at first'. John Cosin could probably have told them that their first approach was doomed to failure.

The restoration of the cathedral was speeded along by Cosin's own contributions to the fabric, including much internal woodwork, such as choir-stalls, an elaborate font-cover and ornate screens.

As for the cathedral library, the dean and prebendaries explained that they had recently bought many more books, so that the old catalogue was now out of date. 'A better is intended and begun to be made': but did they only begin to compile a new catalogue after they had read the bishop's questions? 'As for the books embezzled,' they went on, 'we have and do enquire after them, and have recovered some'.

A copy of Gerard's *Herbal*, a botanical book first published in 1597, had been stolen, along with other treasures, by Isaac Gilpin, the under-master of the cathedral grammar school. He had lent the *Herbal* to Colonel Robert Lilburne, an eminent civil war soldier on the Parliamentary side, and a brother of the Leveller leader John Lilburne. Robert Lilburne, Cosin's correspondents explained, 'is now in the Tower, and still detains the said book from the church's library'. The first edition of John Gerard's *Herbal, or General History of Plants* had run to nearly fifteen hundred pages, many of them illustrated. The dean and prebendaries of Durham claimed that their missing copy had cost ten pounds.

It seems that the cathedral officials had taken Cosin's mention of persons 'known, famed, or suspected, to live in any grievous or scandalous crime' to be a reference to specific people who had committed offences 'punishable by ecclesiastical censures'. They protested that 'the sacrilegious persons here inquired of we cannot yet find out, though your Lordship [meaning the bishop himself] hath put us in hope of finding out one of them'.

As we have seen, John Cosin ran a tight ship where his own money was concerned; even the coins distributed among the poor on his travels were carefully numbered and entered in the accounts. Responding to Cosin's articles, the dean and prebendaries of Durham Cathedral admitted that they could not give the kind of fine-grained financial detail that their bishop requested of them: 'we cannot think that your Lordship expects an exact and full accompt from every one of us, upon oath, of all the monies that we have received and disbursed since our first restoration'.

They protested that some of them had not been in post long, and could not have an exact idea of what was spent by their predecessors. 'It is not unknown to your Lordship,' they went on, 'that our auditor . . . is a person in no way helpful to us in such matters'. The dean and precentors professed that 'we do not believe that your Lordship makes this enquiry out of any distrust of our care of the occasions of the church, or an opinion that we have converted any part of that which is due to them to the private benefit of ourselves and our relations, but rather, as your Lordship hath been pleased to express, that you might be able to give an answer to any that should object such things to us, if any such should be, which we hope there will not'.

Sufferings

Cosin's visitation articles and his many letters concerning the business of his bishopric often give the distinct impression that he was not an easy man to work for or with. He was impatient and suspicious, and expected to get his own way. He worked hard, and had a distinct sense of his own role and powers, which meant that he was bound to be at loggerheads, from time to time, with lesser mortals who refused to give up their entire lives to work.

Some of Cosin's tetchiness can no doubt be attributed to the fact that for many years he was tormented by pain from a number of physical ailments. He suffered from kidney-stone, which led to a torturous symptom called strangury. This meant that Cosin often felt a strong desire to urinate, but was only able to produce a few drops, the passing of which would have caused him great pain. In his short biography of the bishop, C.J. Stranks suggests that Cosin may also have had prostate problems, which would have meant that the bishop had a lot of pain and discomfort concentrated in a small area.

Modern medicine can deploy a reassuring battery of treatments against kidney stone, the probable cause of Cosin's painful strangury, but seventeenth-century medics were of less help. John Gerard, author of the aforementioned *Herbal*, knew of the symptom, describing it as 'when a man cannot piss but by drops', and recommended several herbs, including saxifrage or rockfoil.

Cosin thought that bad weather brought on his strangury, and wrote from London in February 1669 that 'frost and snow and the bitterness of cold . . . hath kept me now this five days together in frequent fits of the strangury, the bitterest pain that ever I felt'.

The bishop also believed that his smoking habit relieved some of his symptoms. In those days, most English smokers used small white-clay pipes, which were an early example of a disposable product. Their narrow stems were easily broken, and archaeological digs in sites from this period often turn up many such pipes. They were sold on street-corners, ready-loaded with tobacco and expertly lit for the convenience of the customer. Some of the bodies of the Scottish soldiers discovered under the disused courtyard among Durham university's Palace Green buildings in 2013 showed signs of inveterate pipe-smoking: teeth in the lower jaws of some of these men had worn down, forming an ugly socket where the pipe rested.

Cosin was evidently all too aware of how easily clay pipes could break, and he bought them a gross at a time; meaning that he paid three shillings, or about twenty pounds in modern money, for a hundred and forty-four at a time. He also paid four shillings a pound for the finest Virginia tobacco.

The bishop was not alone among his contemporaries in thinking that tobacco was a useful medicine. John Gerard wrote that it could be used against a long list of ailments, including migraine, gout, toothache, insomnia, asthma, hoarseness, stomach pains, poor eyesight, deafness, piles, sciatica and a range of skin problems including acne, ulcers and scabs.

Gerard also recommended tobacco as a treatment for a range of wounds, including those caused by arrows and gun-shots. He believed that 'burnings and scaldings' could be helped by the application of tobacco, though he seems to have been wary of the habit of smoking it, preferring to prescribe tobacco juice to be drunk by his patients, or tobacco leaves in various preparations applied externally in the form of ointments or poultices. His cure for burns, including burns caused by a lightning-strike, involved tobacco boiled up with hog's grease and the juice of thorn-apple leaves.

The seventeenth century also had its tobacco sceptics, the most famous of whom was King James I. In his 1604 pamphlet *The*

Counterblast to Tobacco his majesty referred to the smoking habit as a 'base', 'vile' and 'hurtful' 'corruption' and abuse. According to King James, tobacco smoking 'was first found out by some of the barbarous Indians'. The royal author begs his countrymen to refrain from imitating 'the barbarous and beastly manners of the wild, godless, and slavish Indians, especially in so vile and stinking a custom'. As well as tobacco, James particularly disliked Sir Walter Ralegh, whom he calls 'a father so generally hated' and blames for being 'the first author' of smoking among the British. The author of the *Counterblast* reminds his readers that this 'first author' of British smoking, whom he never directly names, was neither a 'king, great conqueror, nor learned doctor of physic'.

Sometimes in *The Counterblast* James seems to be swimming desperately upstream against the strong current of medical opinion, which, as we have seen, favoured tobacco as a cure for many ailments. How can tobacco be a cure for everything? James asks. If it is such a wonderful panacea, then why do so many perfectly healthy young people use it? How can it be healthy, when we know that some users have died from too much smoking?

Much of the medical theory of the time was based on the old idea of the four humours, themselves derived from the notion that many natural things, including people, were made up of a mixture of the 'elements' of earth, air, fire and water. On this basis, doctors would characterise diseases and medicines as, for example, hot and moist, or cold and dry. Seventeenth-century physicians observed that tobacco was hot and dry: they therefore thought that the smoking of it was an excellent antidote to the coolness and moistness of the human brain. But the brain, King James argued, is naturally cool and moist – this quality should not be regarded as a medical condition that needs to be cured.

James I's dislike of tobacco was inherited by his heir King Charles I, a fact which led to a striking incident that may have occurred when Charles visited Durham in 1647. According to a local legend, as recounted by James Raine in his book about Auckland Castle, a lady called Mrs Wren visited the king at Bishop Auckland, and found him in a sort of guard-room surrounded by soldiers, all smoking their heads off. Remembering that her sovereign hated the smell of tobacco, she went around snapping the pipes of the soldiers. Charles commented that 'she had done more than he durst have done'.

Given his heavy smoking, his punishing workload and the poor state of medicine at the time, it is remarkable that John Cosin lived to be as old as he was at the time of his death. In those days in England, life expectancy at birth was under forty, though this figure was distorted by the high rate of infant mortality. Even the figure for life expectancy at thirty – fifty-nine – was tragically low by modern western standards. Part of Cosin's work involved frequent trips away from Durham, which sometimes caused him agony and must also have had a deleterious effect on his health. His friend the Jersey man and Durham Cathedral prebend Jean Durel wrote that in his last days, in London, the old bishop would fall 'into a relapse, which would keep him in his chamber for a good time after' if the motion of his coach or a blast of cold air upset him. A slave to his restless spirit, he would venture out again as soon as his symptoms subsided a little, though 'his friends and physicians' advised him not to go out 'for fear of hazarding the return of his pain'. A planned return to the north was, however, frequently put off.

Durel tells us that in his last months Cosin suffered pain nearly every day, lost his appetite, slept little and breathed with difficulty. In his very last days, the doctors dosed Cosin against the pain and bound his head tightly to suppress a pain there. This medical turban the bishop asked to have undone so that he could take the sacrament uncovered, on his last day. Later he blessed everyone present, including those of his children and grandchildren who were in attendance, and took it into his head that it was a Sunday, and that he was keeping everyone in the room from attending church. About half an hour after he had taken the sacrament, Cosin died without pain, just as if he were falling asleep. His last word was 'Lord'. The immediate cause of his death was thought to have been 'pectoral dropsy', a deadly build-up of fluid in the chest.

The poor state of the roads in winter meant that Cosin's body had to be embalmed in London, and did not leave the bishop's lodgings in Pall Mall until April the nineteenth. On Saturday April the twenty-seventh, John Cosin made his final crossing of the River Tees, which he had first crossed as bishop in 1661, when he was presented with the fabled falchion 'wherewith the champion Conyers slew the worm, dragon, or fiery flying serpent'. This time, 'the greater part of the gentry, with many of the clergy' turned out to honour the remains of the late bishop.

They accompanied Cosin's coffin to Durham Castle, then to the city's cathedral, to which it was attended by the occupants of his almshouses in Durham and Auckland, together with his servants; and gentlemen, esquires and knights dressed in mourning. The bishop of Bristol was in attendance, as were the sheriff of the county, the mayor and aldermen, and four prebends of the cathedral. After a short stay in Durham Cathedral, John Cosin's body was interred in his chapel at Auckland Castle.

The funeral service was conducted by the bishop of Bristol, and a sermon read by Isaac Basire, one of the Durham prebends. Basire's sermon was later published in an expanded form with the title *The Dead Man's Real Speech*, and remains a useful source of information on Cosin's life. If the printed version is anything to go by, Basire's sermon was, however, a remarkably laboured, pedantic and evasive address, full of repetition, irrelevancies, Latin and Greek tags, references to obscure authors, and creaking rhetoric. After warning his hearers against speaking ill of the dead, Basire did manage to praise the late bishop's hospitality, patience, loyalty, hard work, wisdom, learning, punctuality, orderliness, charity, piety and nobility, among other qualities.

Cosin had hoped to be the first person to be buried in his Auckland chapel, but during his absence in London his second daughter had buried her husband, Samuel Davison, in that place. In April 1671 the bishop wrote to his secretary that 'truly you had no reason either to bury him there or elsewhere in the chapel till I had been first consulted, for I never gave my daughter leave to dispose either of house or chapel at her pleasure or any body else but my own'. He added that everyone he spoke to about it in London thought it was 'a sudden and a rash act to suffer any one to be buried there before myself; but since Mr Davenport and my daughter, together with yourself, have thus clapped up the matter, which cannot be now undone again, I must be content to let it be as it is, and say *Requiescat in pace*' (Davenport was Cosin's chaplain).

Cosin in the Balance

In the summer of 1888, over two hundred years after John Cosin was interred under the flagstones of his chapel in Auckland Castle, the place was re-consecrated and a sermon read by the then bishop of Durham, Joseph Barber Lightfoot. Lightfoot's sermon was heard by no less than fifty-seven of his fellow-bishops, from various parts of the British empire including Canada and India, and also the United States. The bishop of Durham's sermon on this occasion was printed in 1892, three years after Lightfoot's death, under the title 'John Cosin' in a book of his sermons called *Leaders in the Northern Church*.

Although he was standing in his chapel, Lightfoot evidently did not feel the need to use his sermon to shower praise on John Cosin. He did not criticise him much either – at least not directly. The scholarly Lightfoot, an important theologian and prolific author, chose instead to criticise Cosin's times, which this Victorian bishop said could not be dwelt on 'without much pain'. As we have seen, the churchmen of Cosin's Arminian party threw in their lot with the monarchy, a choice which Lightfoot characterised as a travesty. Those Stuart clerics believed 'in the divine right of kings, even of tyrants' which, Lightfoot asserted, meant that Anglicanism was subsequently thought of as 'the church of absolutism'. Lightfoot was not the only one who thought that this link between the king and the church was unnecessarily close during the Stuart period. No doubt turning to his American colleagues as he said so, Lightfoot remarked that 'our gathering today is evidence that the Anglican type of Christianity belongs not to any one form of government or any one cast of politics, but can flourish alike under a well-ordered republic and under a constitutional monarchy'.

The drift of Lightfoot's sermon suggests that he believed that if Cosin's type of church was at fault for putting itself under the feet of the Stuart monarchs, the monarchs themselves were at fault in the way they used their power over the church. 'Never had monarch greater opportunities than Charles the Second,' Lightfoot asserted; 'never did monarch abuse his opportunities more miserably and shamefully'. The bishop was no doubt thinking of the persecution of the sects that Charles allowed, which, as we have seen, was energetically pursued by bishops like Cosin. Lightfoot tells us that 'we must hang our heads in shame' to think how little generosity, patience, forbearance, sympathy, love and Christian spirit was shown by Cosin's brothers in arms towards their opponents.

Lightfoot evidently believed that not every sectarian could have been 'comprehended', or included under the Anglican wing, but surely 'if time had been given, if sympathy had been shown, if relief had been afforded, if temporary concessions had been made' the English church could have minimised 'the exclusion of so much piety, so much learning, so much conscientious self-sacrifice'. Here Lightfoot was probably thinking of the Savoy Conference of 1661, and Cosin's participation in it.

Cosin's successor went on to explain that the Anglicans' failure 'to conciliate in place of exasperating' could be attributed in part to the fact that the Restoration, with its oppressive Act of Uniformity, Conventicles Act and Five Miles Act, was 'the age of reprisals'. Churchmen like Cosin had been forced out of their profession, literally 'turned out of house and home': 'their characters had been blackened; their liturgy had been prohibited; their common worship forbidden'. 'When the turn of the political wheel placed them utmost,' Lightfoot went on, 'they forgot the lessons of forgiveness and charity which the Gospel should have taught them'. As we have seen in Judge Jeffreys' words in court to Richard Baxter, many not only wanted to see the Puritans and other sectaries suppressed: they also suspected that if they were not suppressed they might stage another rebellion and return to power: 'don't let us be gulled twice in an age,' Jeffreys had bellowed.

From the perspective of the unusually cold summer of 1888, Lightfoot reminds us that Cosin's chapel at Auckland Castle was consecrated during the oppressive heat of the summer of 1665: a season that brought out the plague and all its horrors, not just in London but in Durham as well. In a letter published by Ornsby, the dean of Carlisle wrote that:

. . . one house is shut up in Durham, in a place they call Crossgate, upon suspicion; and the fear in this place is great, because so many from London and strangers have in the night been observed to resort hither within this week, but now strict watch is commanded to be kept at all common passages about the town, to prevent for the future any entrance by suspected persons.

Cosin was active in raising money in response to this crisis, and also raised funds to help people who had lost everything in the Great Fire of London of 1666.

Lightfoot attempted to weigh Cosin's charitable works in the balance against his sometimes tyrannical actions and his 'unlovely' 'acerbity of temper'. The Restoration bishop's suppression of local sectaries, including Quakers like John Langstaff, is likely to tilt the balance sharply against Cosin, at least in the judgement of modern Christians who embrace ecumenism, and value our wider multi-faith society.

The tragic results of the persecution of sectaries and Roman Catholics by the likes of John Cosin can be read as a warning from history that is relevant to our own age. At present it seems that political and religious opinion is dangerously polarised in many parts of the world, and in some places religion, politics and prejudice are being used as justifications for crass intolerance and callous violence. Regime change happens, and the new leaders waste time unpicking the good things the last regime did, out of blind dogmatism. At the same time, they forget the promises that got them into power in the first place. Genuine dialogue is often replaced by personal insults and baseless accusations, and paranoia takes the place of rational planning. Hard-won rights are sacrificed on the altar of national security, and history is twisted into a shape that suits the ruling class.

Like his tireless efforts to squeeze money out of his diocese, his grand building projects, his charitable works, his work on the Book of Common Prayer and his encouragement of learning, Cosin's harassment of innocent locals who just happened to disagree with him about religion can be seen as part of the bishop's over-arching project to glorify the English church which he believed that he and his comrades were working to restore to its rightful position. Cosin's successful attempt to frustrate the people of Durham's aspirations to elect their own members of parliament was probably motivated by a similar feeling. That he believed that the Church of England could not shine out in all its glory if rival churches were blocking some of the light is probably a function of Cosin's own brand of national and religious loyalty, and was entirely typical of his age. It is not given to everyone to float above the stream of history and see things, as Cosin's younger contemporary Baruch Spinoza tried to do, *sub specie aeternitatis*; from the point of view of eternity.

Select Bibliography

Aubrey, John: *Thomas Hobbes*, Langley Press, 2016

Bayne, A.D.: *A Comprehensive History of Norwich*, Jarrold, 1869

Baxter, Richard: *The Autobiography of Richard Baxter*, Dent, 1974

Baxter, Richard: *The Life of Rev. Richard Baxter, Chiefly compiled from his own writings*, Scholarly Publishing Office, University of Michigan Library, 2005

Baxter, Richard: *A Paraphrase on the New Testament*, B. and T. Simmons, 1685

Baxter, Richard: *The Reformed Pastor*, Banner of Truth, 1974

Besse, Joseph: *A Collection of the Sufferings of the People Called Quakers*, Luke Hinde, 1753

Billings, R.W.: *Illustrations of the Architectural Antiquities of the County of Durham*, George Andrews, 1846

Bradshaw, Paul F.: *The Anglican Ordinal*, SPCK, 1971

Braithwaite, William C.: *The Second period of Quakerism*, William Sessions, 1979

Brickstock, Richard: *Durham Castle*, Jeremy Mills, 2007

Carlton, C.M: *History of the Charities in the City of Durham*, George Walker, 1872

Christology: Agreed Statement by the Anglican-Oriental Orthodox International Commission 2014, Anglican Consultative Council, 2015

Cosin, John: *A Collection of Private Devotions*, Oxford, 1967

Cosin, John: *The Correspondence of John Cosin* (2 vols.), Andrews, 1869

Cragg, Gerald R.: *The Church and the Age of Reason*, Penguin, 1970

Cuming, Geoffrey: *The Godly Order*, SPCK, 1983

Cummings, Brian: *The Book of Common Prayer*, Oxford, 2011

Dowsing, William: *The Journal of William Dowsing*, Boydell, 2001

Edwards, G.F.: *Auckland Castle*

Evelyn, John: *The Diary of John Evelyn*, Everyman, 2006

Fox, George: *The Journal of George Fox*, Dent, 1924

Gameson, Richard (ed.): *Treasures of Durham University Library*, Third Millennium, 2007

Gerard, John: *The Herbal or General History of Plants*, Dover, 2015

Halliday, F.E.: *A Shakespeare Companion*, Penguin, 1964

Henderson, William: *Notes on the Folk-Lore of the Northern Counties of England and the Borders*, Folk-Lore Society, 1879

Hickes, George: *The Spirit of Enthusiasm Exorcised*, Walter Kettilby, 1680

Hierurgia Anglicana (ed. Camden Soc.), Rivington & Masters, 1848

Hobbes, Thomas: *Leviathan*, Penguin, 2017

Jacobs, Alan: *The Book of Common Prayer: a Biography*, Princeton University Press, 2013

Johnson, Margot (ed.): *John Cosin*, Turnstone, 1997

Kelly, Mike: *Shakespeare and Love*, Ashgrove, 2014

Lightfoot, J.B.: *Leaders in the Northern Church*, Macmillan, 1892

Longstaff, George Blundell: *The Langstaffs of Teesdale and Weardale*, M. Hughes and Clarke, 1923

Mémoires de Messire Gaspar de Colligny, Oliphant, 1844

Millward, J.S. (ed.): *Portraits and Documents: Seventeenth Century*, Hutchinson, 1961

Mountagu, Richard: *Appello Caesarem*, Matthew Lownes, 1625

Mountagu, Richard: *A Gag for the New Gospel? No: a New Gag for an Old Goose,* printed by Thomas Snodham for Matthew Lownes and William Barret, 1624

More, Paul Elmer and Cross, Frank Leslie (eds.): *Anglicanism*, SPCK, 1935

Osmond, P.H.: *A Life of John Cosin*, Mowbray, 1913

Pearce, Dominic: *Henrietta Maria*, Amberley, 2015

Penn, W.A.: *The Soverane Herbe: A History of Tobacco*, Grant Richards, 1902

Powicke, F.J.: *A Life of the Reverend Richard Baxter*, Houghton Mifflin, 1924

Procter, Francis and Frere, Walter Howard (eds.): *A New History of the Book of Common Prayer*, Macmillan, 1961

Prynne William: *Canterbury's Doom*, Michael Spark, 1646

Prynne, William: *Histriomastix*, London, 1632

Raine, James: *A Brief Historical Account of the Episcopal Castle, or Palace, of Auckland*, George Andrews, 1852

Rutherford, Moira: *Quakers in the City of Durham, 1654-1858*, White & Co., 1997

Sharp, Cuthbert: *The Bishoprick Garland: Or, A Collection of Legends, Songs, Ballads, &c. Belonging to the County of Durham*, Nichols, and Baldwin & Cradock, 1834

Smart, Peter: *A Sermon Preached in the Cathedral Church of Durham, July 7 1628*, London, 1640

Southcombe, George and Tapsell, Grant: *Restoration Politics, Religion and Culture*, Palgrave Macmillan, 2010

Sparrow, Anthony: *A Rationale upon the Book of Common Prayer*, London, 1672

Stranks, C.J.: *John Cosin: Restorer of the Bishoprick 1660-1672*, Durham Cathedral, 1978

Stranks, C.J.: *This Sumptuous Church*, SPCK, 1973

Stuart, James (King James I): *The Counterblast to Tobacco*, Putnam, 1905

Venn, John: *College Histories: Caius College*, Robinson & Co., 1901

Webb, Simon: *The Dunbar Martyrs*, Langley Press, 2017

Webb, Simon: *In Search of Bede*, Langley Press, 2016

Webb, Simon: *In Search of the Little Count*, Langley Press, 2008

Webb, Simon: *The Life and Times of John Duck*, Langley Press, 2019

Webb, Simon: *The Prince Bishops of Durham*, Langley Press, 2013

Wickham Legg, L.G. (ed.) *A Relation of a Short Survey of 26 Counties*, Robinson, 1904

For free downloads and more from the Langley Press,
please visit our website at http://tinyurl.com/lpdirect